FEATURES

AUTUMN 2023 • NUMBER 37

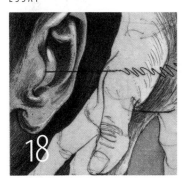
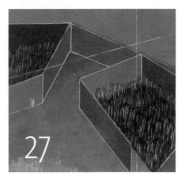

Plough

INSIGHTS

DEPARTMENTS

WEB EXCLUSIVES

Plough

ANOTHER LIFE IS POSSIBLE

EDITOR: Peter Mommsen
SENIOR EDITORS: Shana Goodwin, Maria Hine, Maureen Swinger, Sam Hine, Susannah Black Roberts
EDITOR-AT-LARGE: Caitrin Keiper
BOOKS AND CULTURE EDITOR: Joy Marie Clarkson
POETRY EDITOR: A. M. Juster
DESIGNERS: Rosalind Stevenson, Miriam Burleson
CREATIVE DIRECTOR: Clare Stober
COPY EDITORS: Wilma Mommsen, Priscilla Jensen
FACT CHECKER: Suzanne Quinta
MARKETING DIRECTOR: Trevor Wiser
UK EDITION: Ian Barth
CONTRIBUTING EDITORS: Leah Libresco Sargeant, Brandon McGinley, Jake Meador, Madoc Cairns
FOUNDING EDITOR: Eberhard Arnold (1883–1935)
Plough Quarterly No. 37: The Enemy
Published by Plough Publishing House, ISBN 978-1-63608-095-6
Copyright © 2023 by Plough Publishing House. All rights reserved.

EDITORIAL OFFICE
151 Bowne Drive
Walden, NY 12586
T: 845.572.3455
info@plough.com

SUBSCRIBER SERVICES
PO Box 8542
Big Sandy, TX 75755
T: 800.521.8011
subscriptions@plough.com

United Kingdom
Brightling Road
Robertsbridge
TN32 5DR
T: +44(0)1580.883.344

Australia
4188 Gwydir Highway
Elsmore, NSW
2360 Australia
T: +61(0)2.6723.2213

Plough Quarterly (ISSN 2372-2584) is published quarterly by Plough Publishing House, PO Box 398, Walden, NY 12586.
Individual subscription $36 / £24 / €28 per year.
Subscribers outside of the United States and Canada pay in British pounds or euros.
Periodicals postage paid at Walden, NY 12586 and at additional mailing offices.
POSTMASTER: Send address changes to Plough Quarterly, PO Box 8542, Big Sandy, TX 75755.

Front cover: *The Snake Charmer*, statue by Charles Arthur Bourgeois, 1863.
    Photograph by neko92vl. Used by permission.
Inside front cover: Rashid al-Din Tabib, *Yunus [Jonah] and the Whale*, ca. 1314. Used by permission.
Back cover: Piet Mondrian, *Apple Tree, Pointillist Version*, ca. 1908. Public domain.

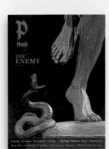

ABOUT THE COVER

Since the Garden of Eden, snakes have been perceived as the enemy – sometimes lashing out, sometimes whispering suggestions into the listener's ear. This striking sculpture could represent the devil at our heels, or the enemy within.

LETTERS

READERS RESPOND

Readers respond to *Plough's* Summer 2023 issue, *Money*. Send letters to *letters@plough.com*.

THE SPIRIT OF MAMMON

On Eugene McCarraher's "Enchanted Capitalism": I was hesitant to read your "Money" issue. Perhaps my hesitancy is based upon fear. Fear that the magazine's articles would hammer down too hard and shatter my hard-earned assumptions about money.

But then I read portions of the "Money" issue. Nothing was shattered. But I certainly started thinking, and thinking.

Today I'm still thinking about Eugene McCarraher's definition of "mammon." Unfortunately, I have never taken the time to properly exegete this term, even confusing mammon with money. But McCarraher points out that mammon is a spirit, the spirit of acquisition, the spirit of ruthlessness.

Though money is certainly a coveted commodity for this ruthless spirit of acquisition, money is not the same thing as mammon. McCarraher states that according to the New Testament, mammon is "a demon who encourages greed, stupidity, endless dissatisfaction, all for the purposes of endless acquisition." Mammon is a spiritual force. No wonder Jesus said that we cannot serve both God and mammon.

D. R. Groten, Spring Valley, Minnesota

WHAT IS MONEY FOR?

On Peter Mommsen's "The Other Side of the Needle's Eye": This essay tugs at the heartstrings so. I admire how truths are brought to light as gently as if they were mere suggestions, how the rebuttal to some of Augustine's conclusions is structured and exposited. I personally would make a passionate mess of it.

What the essay did with such force, however, was bring me to a reflection on my own hypocrisy and self-righteousness. Being from a Third World African country, I realize that I would be first to champion the true teaching of selflessness concerning wealth, as directed by the Bible. But then, to think of how rich Pinianus and Melania were, I couldn't help but harbor a resentment for what they did. Having known the nature of poverty in a materialistic society, I find that I envy what they had but not in any way what they did. A part of me lies that I would have served God better having the wealth with me than giving it all away. And so, I pray for grace and strength.

Isaac Kilibwa, Vihiga, Western Kenya

On Maureen Swinger's "On Owning Twenty-Two Cars": Interesting glimpse into one who is not dominated by frivolous wants, but who nevertheless lives securely in the knowledge that genuine needs will be taken care of.

That security must be comforting, but in today's consumption-driven society, it is hard to imagine living without money. Only one committed to a higher ideal and to "live simply so that others might simply live" will be able to sustain that ideal.

Ann Dayton, St Ives, Cornwall, United Kingdom

AGAINST USURY

On Readings, "Where Your Treasure Is": As C. S. Lewis famously said in *Mere Christianity*, three major ancient thought systems — Greek, Christian, and Jewish — considered usury unethical.

How could we have such amnesia? Or is it deafness or blindness? Saint Paul put it well, "The good that I would do, I do not, and the evil that I would not do, I do."

Most Americans can't imagine the possibility that we stole land from Native Americans or enslaved people for centuries, so compelled are we to think of ourselves as good people. Well. Why not make money on money?

The role of money runs so deep — in our land use, governmental systems, work systems, and personal daily habits — that it is hard to overrate it. Or oversee it. Or see over it. We blame the poor for their poverty and honor the rich for their wealth — and even have prosperity "gospels."

What does this mean? We are not who we think we are, nor are we capable of being much different. We are, early and often, misshapen. We hide truth in plain sight.

If we start there, we might have an angle on how unimportant money is compared to personal coherence. Truth in lending? Future results not based on past performance? Shedding the skin of righteousness would be a great place to start to get into a right relationship with money.

Donna Schaper, West Haven, Connecticut

UNLIKELY SAMARITANS

On Phil Christman's "The Effective Samaritan," plough.com: Given the logic of the parable, anyone stopping to help would thereby be neighbor to the victim, however improbable or contrived, whether Samaritan, effective altruist, or Kanye West. Nevertheless, ethical commitments matter, and in reality a consistent effective altruist would be the least likely of the passersby to help, given the signature rationalization that one's time and money secure greater overall benefit if donated to nonlocal causes, like prevention of improbable distant future existential threats to humanity. Yet I suppose that while with man this story is impossible, with God all things are possible.

Paul Nedelisky, Charlottesville, Virginia

On Myron Glick's "Who Deserves Medical Care?" plough.com: I spent over thirty-six years in the legal profession. Part of our responsibility as practicing attorneys was to give back to the community – to do some pro bono work – for the common good.

Some were better at this than others, but every one of us knew of this responsibility. Why is there not the same attitude among healthcare professionals? Though I hear of some doctors – such as the one in this story – I never hear of the medical profession as a whole determining that it is up to them to be part of the solution. My father was a country doctor back when they still made house calls – and certainly would always help those in need and never turn someone away just because he or she couldn't pay. If more doctors were like this, we wouldn't have this national crisis.

R. Neely Owen, Merrill, Wisconsin

THE PRICELESS CAFÉ

On Robert Lockridge's "Pay As You Can": As with any real attempt to live in community,

there is nearly always one or more people who seem bent on "taking advantage" of generosity, of taking far more than they seem willing to give. This type is often called a "freeloader." This is especially difficult in your situation, the "pay what you can" mixture of charity and commerce.

Perhaps the difficulty lies in the direct mixture of two fairly incompatible ways of handling the basic needs of people. Commerce is based on real expectation of some level of profit, of financial gain in the process. Charity seeks no financial gain whatsoever, but is supposed to be altruistic by nature. It might be true that only perfected people could properly navigate a "pay as you can" system. It becomes a playground for moral compromise unless those participating actually have a strong moral compass already functioning.

In this story, when Kevin was exposed as a "user" type, he disappeared, along with his happy-go-lucky facade. Perhaps he really

needed the charity, but just as likely not. I genuinely admire your guts to attempt such a venture, and my own community of believers has discussed doing similar things. I'm just not sure we can mix charity and commerce.

Andrew J. Churney, Pal Coast, Florida

A WHISTLEBLOWER'S LEGACY

On Robert Ellsberg's "A Father's Legacy to His Son – and His Country," plough.com: A moving tribute from a highly thoughtful and articulate son about a father who was not the stereotypical baseball-tossing, sports-cheering dad. So many compelling questions: Did the stern choices he made in his life's work make a difference? Yes, at some level, and probably no: here we are, decades later, mired in much the same problems.

Thank you to author and subject for this thought-provoking profile of one of tormented twentieth-century America's significant actors.

Kristine Montamat, Charlottesville, Virginia

NOT WALKING AWAY

On Michelle Van Loon's "A Good Death for Dying Churches," plough.com: What if we didn't have the luxury of walking (or running) away from disagreement, or cherry-picking services? What if our spiritual survival depended on getting along, working through problems, clinging to one another, even in conflict, as if the people around us were the only ones

who understood us and knew what we're up against? How many priorities would change if walking away weren't an option? I think the most logical and biblical organization for the church is "how far do you want to walk?" I don't do this; I drive by two churches to get to a specific church, like most Christians I know. And I've seen two splits in my short time, like the one described in this article. There's something compelling and biblical about the idea of not being allowed to walk away faultless – like family. You can stop talking to family, but it never goes away.

Scott Kenney, Colorado Springs, Colorado

WHEN FAITH BRINGS UNCERTAINTY

On Alan Noble's "Living with Religious Scrupulosity or Moral OCD," plough.com: I appreciate this thoughtful piece. I am also a practicing Christian who has experienced OCD for many years, including the variety described here. As the author indicates, one of the biggest hurdles in treating moral scrupulosity is becoming comfortable with uncertainty. I have learned to accept a fair degree of grey in the moral decision-making process, all under the overriding belief that God truly loves me. This entails living with the possibility that I might be wrong: God may be dissatisfied with the extent of my repentance, my avoidance of sinful behaviors, etc. The key is listening to what my gut says is true about the gospel and trusting that God loves me despite my incomplete obedience.

Steven Marquardt, Tucker, Georgia

When Love Seems Impossible

Working in war zones tests my commitment to nonviolence daily. It's the refugees who show me the way.

Oddny Gumaer

Doing relief work in Bangladesh, Iraq, and Ukraine, I get this feeling sometimes: a wave of nausea comes over me and I know that if I don't walk away quickly and focus elsewhere, I will start crying uncontrollably. The pain, sorrow, and desperation of people I have met fill my heart and suddenly there is no more space. I cannot hear one more story of grief, loss, and suffering; I cannot face another mother, father, or child who is a victim of the world's brutality.

It's not my pain I feel; it's theirs. Then it is the feeling of inadequacy, of being powerless to fix their lives or fix the world.

One day I saw a woman screaming in Mosul. It felt like we were in a postapocalyptic world. A town in complete ruins, dust still settling. People wandering about, looking lost. But this woman wouldn't stop screaming. I couldn't understand her words, but something drew me to her. "Why is she screaming?" I asked.

They told me she was going crazy because some days ago, her house had collapsed when a bomb hit it, and her four sons were buried underneath. They were still there. Dead now. She wanted somebody to help her uncover them to give them a proper burial.

"We don't have the time to rescue the dead," they told her. "Our time must be spent saving the living."

She screamed again. I thought about how I would have acted had it been my three daughters buried under the ruins of my home. I would have acted crazy, just like her. So I put my arms around her. The only thing I knew how to do. She pushed me away and walked on, still screaming.

Faced with such horrors, there are times when I want the perpetrators to die, painfully. I get an intense urge to make these people suffer for their crimes. It seems we are hardwired for such a response: we want revenge when injustice has been committed.

A child in Dahuk, Kurdistan, at a temporary camp for Yazidi refugees.

But my desire for revenge quickly fades. "The old law of an eye for an eye leaves everyone blind," said Martin Luther King Jr. Of course, this is what Jesus said too, telling us not to resist an evil person but to turn the other cheek. Violence begets violence; responding to evil with evil perpetuates an endless cycle of vengeance.

I understand this. I understand it well when I am sitting at home in my living room, where there is no war and nobody is attacking my country or my family. The principles of nonviolence have been part of my identity for years as I marched for peace, lobbied in the halls of power, and fought for democracy by wearing T-shirts with political slogans or signing petitions.

As I encounter a village reduced to rubble, however, the devastation rattles my convictions. Bullet-riddled walls serve as reminders of the brutality endured; a lone teddy bear abandoned in the dirt serves as a symbol of lost childhood. I hear stories of tanks crushing cars for amusement and of soldiers raping girls. In the face of such atrocities, my commitment to nonviolence is tested.

At such times, it has been the victims who have pointed me in the right direction. Once, at a hidden site in the jungles of Myanmar where a group of Rohingya people lived in constant fear of being discovered after their village was burned to the ground by government soldiers, I asked, "Do you hate them?"

Their response was one of bewilderment as they explained, "We cannot hate them, for by doing so, we would become like them." For them, the path to survival was forgiveness.

I asked a Bengali guard why Bangladesh, despite its own economic challenges, chose to accept a substantial number of Rohingya refugees escaping the Myanmar government's genocide. I will never forget his response: "We have endured much suffering ourselves. We understand first-hand the anguish they face. It is natural for us to provide refuge to those who are also struggling with terrible suffering."

Despite ongoing persecution, the Karen people of Myanmar regularly hold thanks-giving services. I asked one of them why they were thankful, if their lives were so miserable. She responded: "There is much to be thankful to God for. We are alive. We had food to eat today. The rains ceased."

During visits to villages in the Donetsk region of Ukraine, I hear similar sentiments. Here unrest has persisted since 2014 and the sound of explosions fills the air throughout the day. "I have cried for days," a young mother of two says. "I am crying because brothers are killing brothers. I do not hate the Russians, and now we are forced to fight them."

A twenty-six-year-old Ukrainian soldier expresses his reluctance to shoot Russians. "I wish they would just go home to their wives and children," he said. "I don't like killing people. The first time I shot a man, it struck me that he, too, was a man just like me." ➤

Oddny Gumaer and her husband, Steve, founded Partners Relief & Development and more recently the Novi Community, whose mission is to restore childhoods disrupted by war. The Gumaers have worked with displaced people in Southeast Asia, the Middle East, and Ukraine.

Left: Oddny and her husband, Steve, next to apartment buildings bombed by the Russian army in Irpin, near Kyiv. *Right:* A child in Kherson, under Russian occupation. This same area was later affected by the collapse of the Kakhovka Dam, which flooded many villages.

Places to Think with Neighbors

Lyceums bring the positive energy of learning to local communities.

Nathan Beacom

In 1826, in Connecticut, a farmer named Josiah Holbrook started a school for "the general diffusion of knowledge and … raising the moral and intellectual taste" of Americans. In those days, the opportunities for higher education were limited to those venerable old universities that had long served the upper crust. Holbrook's vision was to make learning – practical, liberal, and humane – available to working people of all kinds. He named his school the Lyceum, after the garden where Aristotle once taught his students philosophy.

The idea spread like wildfire. Within a few decades, there were thousands of lyceums across the country, representing a thriving intellectual life in large cities and small country towns. Abraham Lincoln gave his first public speech at a lyceum in Springfield, Illinois. Frederick Douglass, Mark Twain, Susan B. Anthony, and all the great thinkers of the day toured the lyceum circuit, putting their ideas in dialogue with ordinary Americans. Henry David Thoreau wrote for his local lyceum in Concord. When Alexander Graham Bell debuted the telephone, it was at a lyceum. In Jefferson, Iowa, or Brookline, Massachusetts, you could find working folks listening to lectures on anthropology, philosophy, politics, and more.

And then the lyceum disappeared. Communities broke apart in the Gilded Age as families moved and shifted toward big cities. Individualism replaced the communal learning of the past and social Darwinism became the new philosophy du jour. In reaction to growing individualism and weakening community life, grassroots organizations, like the Rotary Club, Kiwanis Club, Lions, and others, were formed to knit communities back together. Protestant Americans emphasized the "social gospel," and Catholics introduced the language of "social justice." Lyceums, too, saw a revival in the form of the public forum movement. These and other factors contributed to historically high levels of social trust and civic participation in the middle of the twentieth century.

But, as social scientist Robert Putnam famously documented in *Bowling Alone*, social cohesion, community engagement, and community trust have plummeted across a wide array of measures since that time, and these things have taken a nosedive from the 1990s to now. People report fewer conversations with neighbors, fewer friendships, less engagement in community organizations and civic life, and a growing distrust of their fellow Americans. Coincident with all this, our engagement with ideas has moved away from a public forum with neighbors and toward TV and social media, where the humanizing element of physical proximity is lost. No longer are we in the scrum of intellectual engagement with those with whom we live; instead, we are locked in our own angry echo chambers online, growing ever more extreme and unable to sympathize with those unlike us.

In this environment, the Lyceum Movement has launched an effort to bring back this forum for conversation and learning. In its time, the lyceum was a way for neighbors to form relationships around a common pursuit of learning. This is eminently good for a community. In the process of shared learning and intellectual exploration, trust and shared understanding grow, and a habit of cooperation in search of a shared good, the good of knowledge, is formed.

In the midst of a confusing turmoil of online noise, the lyceum offers a place to think about first principles and about the stories we share. We hold lectures, panels, classes, and community conversations in a relaxed

---

Nathan Beacom, a writer in Chicago, Illinois, is the founder and executive director of the Lyceum Movement. This article is excerpted from The Liberating Arts: Why We Need Liberal Arts Education *(Plough, September 2023).* See page 100.

Alexander Graham Bell demonstrating his experimental telephone, with a connection between Salem and Boston, Massachusetts, in Lyceum Hall, Salem, 1877. Sketch by E. R. Morse.

About Us

Plough is published by the Bruderhof, an international community of families and singles seeking to follow Jesus together. Members of the Bruderhof are committed to a way of radical discipleship in the spirit of the Sermon on the Mount. Inspired by the first church in Jerusalem (Acts 2 and 4), they renounce private property and share everything in common in a life of nonviolence, justice, and service to neighbors near and far. There are twenty-nine Bruderhof settlements in both rural and urban locations in the United States, England, Germany, Australia, Paraguay, South Korea, and Austria, with around 3000 people in all. To learn more or arrange a visit, see the community's website at *bruderhof.com*.

Plough features original stories, ideas, and culture to inspire faith and action. Starting from the conviction that the teachings and example of Jesus can transform and renew our world, we aim to apply them to all aspects of life, seeking common ground with all people of goodwill regardless of creed. The goal of *Plough* is to build a living network of readers, contributors, and practitioners so that, as we read in Hebrews, we may "spur one another on toward love and good deeds."

Plough includes contributions that we believe are worthy of our readers' consideration, whether or not we fully agree with them. Views expressed by contributors are their own and do not necessarily reflect the editorial position of *Plough* or of the Bruderhof communities.

social atmosphere. Human beings have always needed this, whether in the Greek agora or a Boston tavern; we need a place to pursue the fundamental human desire to know with our neighbors.

Since its beginning in 2021, the new Lyceum Movement has grown to a presence in four states and six cities, and it has generated a remarkable amount of positive energy in communities large and small. People are hungry for an alternative to the alienating experience of life online; they're hungry for a substantive conversation with a neighbor.

We take the subjects of the liberal arts and put them in local contexts. In Des Moines, Iowa, we've spoken about virtue ethics by way of a discussion between commodity farmers and farmers focused on sustainability. We've explored questions of human solidarity through dialogue between philosophers and refugees. We've explored local history in places like Duluth, Minnesota, and St. Louis, Missouri. These are subjects many people think about in the quiet moments of their working lives, and they are hungry for an opportunity to develop those thoughts with the help of a scholar or expert and in conversation with their neighbors. This is often true of those who don't suspect that this kind of intellectual talk is for them. Not everyone is an academic, nor should they be, and our events have been places where a farmer, a construction worker, a lawyer, and a schoolteacher can think deeply together.

A healthy common life requires a shared frame of reference, a shared language, and a shared sense of purpose. If we only talk as a community at times of political conflict, we are bound to talk past each other. We

won't have a shared understanding of the very words we are using, we won't have shared stories to point to, and we won't have relationships of trust to ground us. The liberal arts can offer something here. Studying philosophy, literature, and history in community can at least give us a common set of terms, a better understanding of our neighbor's point of view, and a shared frame of reference so that we can fruitfully disagree.

We need to go deeper than the superficial fights that characterize public life. We need to return to first principles and meet each other there as human beings. The lyceum is working to provide a space to do this, with the goal of bringing back the lyceum halls that once served as centers of community learning and thinking for so many towns and cities. Learning in community is not a panacea for our complex problems, but it can help cultivate the soil from which productive work for the common good may grow.

Poet in This Issue

Australian-born poet Stephen Edgar studied classics and librarianship at the University of Tasmania and lived in London before settling in Sydney. Noted for his commitment to formal verse, he has published a dozen collections of poetry and has won numerous Australian awards and honors for poetry, including the Prime Minister's 2021 Literary Award for his recent book *The Strangest Place*. Read his poems "Lammergeier" on page 39, "South Head" on page 55, and "World Within" on page 87.

MAUREEN SWINGER

Thanksgiving Starts in September

*Here's a brief tour of autumn celebrations
at a Bruderhof community.*

*The boughs do shake and the bells do ring,
so merrily comes the harvest in.*

WE USUALLY END UP having at least three Thanksgivings at Fox Hill. The first few are not written onto the calendar, but by September, as the last of the garden bounty rolls in, celebration is in the air. This may be a hark-back to the old English festival of Harvest Home, also known as Ingathering, which I like better, as it gathers people in as well as crops. There are communal games and hayrides in the afternoon; anyone who wants to wear out his or her arms can have a go at cider pressing. For dinner, there may be roasted chicken and roasted vegetables, and roasted . . . well . . . anything else someone is inspired to roast, and buttery golden corn on the cob and fresh salads with the last of the vine-ripe tomatoes. With the long trestle tables and the happy bustle of families and friends swapping small talk and complimenting the dishes, it's rather reminiscent of a Redwall feast.

Sometimes September will bless us with a double bounty, if Bruderhof members who have joined us from South Korea host a Chuseok festival, a celebration of the mid-autumn full

Maureen Swinger is a senior editor at Plough. *She lives at the Fox Hill Bruderhof in Walden, New York, with her husband, Jason, and their three children.*

moon, involving traditional games, music, and rice cakes steamed over pine needles.

These banquets usually end in song – four-part harmonies for all the rich autumnal melodies that welcome the season:

By all these lovely tokens, September days are here
With summer's best of weather,
    and autumn's best of cheer.

Someone will always spoonerize that last line into "autumn's chest of beer," which is more accurate for the next month's celebration:

Oktoberfest! This one reaches back to German roots that most of our folks don't actually share, but that is where it all began for the Bruderhof more than a hundred years ago. So, much as everyone becomes Irish in March, October is our month to break out the craft beer, pull sea-salted supersized soft pretzels out of a brick oven, throw on a sizzling bratwurst, and apply honey mustard liberally.

Last year, the schoolchildren and teachers hosted this event in dirndls and lederhosen, hats and ribbons. Performances might be anything from country dances to folk songs from the old country, such as:

Our joy new we share, throw our hats in the air.
Juheisa! The harvest is in.

If your joy can best be expressed by throwing your hat in the air, now is the time to do it. Oktoberfest isn't just about food; there are often events such as a log-sawing contest, pumpkin toss, obstacle course, or hay-bale maze. Everyone mingles and munches until the sun goes down.

Mid-October is peak fall color in the Hudson Valley, and I love to go down to our wide, shallow lake around sunset, when the maples and the evening sky paint the surface.

The world is full of color, 'tis autumn once again,
And leaves of gold and crimson are lying in the lane.
There's beauty of light and shadow,
    glory of wheat and rye,
And color of shining water under a sunset sky.

Now the dusk falls before the smallest children's bedtime, which means there is one more celebration to fit in – this one firstly a feast for the eyes. Lantern walks are a time-honored Bruderhof tradition; perhaps in the dim mists of time they were connected to the German Saint Martin's Day parade, but now they are just a chance for the children to construct or choose the most creative

Photograph by Tim Clement. Used by permission.

paper lantern (yes, there are real candles inside, small occasional flare-ups notwithstanding) and savor the sight of an entire community wending its sparkling way around the premises, singing songs about lights that hold their own against the autumn dark. As a kid I didn't consider the walk complete unless we circled the pond, so that each side of the parade could see the others' lights reflected and dancing in mirrored patterns. When everyone is cold and hungry, we reconvene in the lantern-lit dining hall for deep-fried homemade doughnuts, dripping in chocolate, caramel, or honey frosting. Then the families drift home – satisfied, sticky, and sleepy.

You'd think we'd be partied out by the time Thanksgiving rolls around, and in a way it is a bit more subdued, as feasts go. November has closed over the fields and the leaves are down. Everything that can be harvested has been; now the good things come out of the freezers and root cellars. Neighbors from the surrounding area often join our community for Thanksgiving dinner, though sometimes we've surprised them by serving roast duck and sauer-kraut. I've never known the cooks to swap out the fresh pumpkin pie for anything else, though.

Last year there was a paper tree on the wall, and a flurry of paper leaves on every table, plus pens. Everyone wrote down something they were thankful for on a leaf (good friends, laughter, roast duck, my favorite teacher, winter soup, Grandpa, Christmas coming). The kids were kept busy all dinner climbing up and down a stepladder to apply them to the twigs, while some leaves became detatched and drifted down onto their heads to muffled giggles.

To me, rather than a family-and-football holiday, Thanksgiving is more of a chance to cast my mind back over the goodness of the year, before turning toward the next great celebration. Advent will be here in a few days; the gatherings and songs of that season have an even more sacred and joyous beauty, and draw us closer together. But for now, it's time to stand under a November sky and hold out a quiet thanks for what has been and what is coming.

On the far horizon the clouds are heaped like snow
And the theater of heaven is bright with sovereign glow,
The bees are filling their hives with a dusty gold,
And the heart is filled with more than a heart can hold.

TIMOTHY J. KEIDERLING

Tough Love *on the* Mount

*Who were those enemies Jesus expected his
oppressed listeners to love?*

SINCE 2021, MY WIFE and daughter and I have been living in Israel, where I've had the privilege of studying the New Testament in depth in the land where much of it took place. More times than I can count I've stood on the Mount of Olives looking out over Jerusalem, wondering what Jesus must have been thinking when he wished that Jerusalem would know "the things that make for peace." I've climbed many hills around the Sea of Galilee (because nobody knows which one he preached from), watched the far-off ripples dance in the sunlight, smelled the spring anemones and mustard and the summertime weeds. Standing where the disciples might have stood and listened to Jesus, I've often tried to imagine hearing Jesus tell them to "love your enemies and do good to those who persecute you" (Matt. 5:44).

In *The Sage from Galilee,* Jewish scholar of Christianity David Flusser notes that Jesus was the only person in the New Testament to give the command to "love your enemies." The silence of other writers, he suggests, exists because the commandment is "very difficult." Praying for your persecutors is one thing, he writes. But loving your enemies? That is Jesus at his most radical.

But when Jesus said "enemy," what did he mean? Whom did he want his disciples to love?

Could he have meant the Pharisees, his frequent theological sparring partners? Of course, Jesus argued with the Pharisees, but sometimes we argue most with those to whom we feel close. His arguments with them sound a lot like those the Pharisees leveled against each other. *Jerusalem Talmud Berakhot* 9:5, which includes a famous list of seven kinds of bad Pharisee, reads "the balancing Pharisee commits one sin and then does one commandment and balances one against the other" (translation mine). Strenuous disagreement does not necessarily imply enmity; as Brad H. Young details in *Jesus the Jewish Theologian,* Jesus shared much with the Pharisees, including his technique of teaching in parables.

On the one hand, it is quite possible that Jesus had in mind the common enemy: the Roman occupiers. There are certain experiences of a nation under occupation that make for common cause among the occupied. The constant presence of soldiers wearing the uniform of a foreign power. The indignities. The paying of taxes. The felt absence of freedom. These things would have been common to all his listeners. And Jesus wasn't making this easy for them. Before asking them point-blank to love their enemies, he had already "triggered" his audience, inviting them to recall a particularly demeaning encounter with an abusive Roman soldier: "If anyone slaps you on the right cheek, turn to him the other cheek also. . . . If anyone forces you to go one mile, go with him two miles" (Matt. 5:39, 41).

A bird's-eye view of the political situation in Roman Palestine in Jesus' time shows that in all likelihood the only people who were not at least frustrated at the Roman occupation were those who stood to benefit monetarily – more on the tax collectors in a moment. The rest, whether in Jerusalem or Galilee, probably didn't like what they saw and wanted it to end. In other words, there would have been a common enemy, and it may well have been Rome. When those in power in Judea took the side of Rome and made alliances, no wonder revolution broke out. An enemy is an enemy.

Timothy Keiderling is a PhD student at the Hebrew University of Jerusalem and a member of the Bruderhof. He lives with his wife and two daughters in Galilee, where he is writing his dissertation.

Cornelius, we read, "gave alms generously." According to Shimon the Righteous, a high priest who lived in the second century BC, the giving of charity is one of the three pillars on which the world stands (Mishnah *Avot* 1:2). All that to say that there were Romans who clearly were not "enemies"; the picture is more complex.

The tax collectors seem to also have been generally regarded as collaborators with the Roman occupation. The first-century Jewish historian Josephus doesn't give much detail about public opinion concerning tax collectors, but he does explain that starting during the time of the Ptolemies (before the Roman conquest) tax collection contracts, so to speak, were given to the highest bidder, and that some rich men in Syria and Egypt who won the bids gained fabulous sums of money (*Antiquities* 12:167). In other words, corruption was rampant around the collection and processing of taxes.

Rabbinic sources give us a better understanding of just how much social ostracism tax collectors experienced. The majority opinion in rabbinic thought, for instance, forbade people to accept charity from a tax collector, because it was assumed that the money was stolen (*Bava Kamma* 113a). Tax collectors were also not allowed to testify in a court of law (Mishnah *Sanhedrin* 3a). Yet Jesus chose a tax collector as a disciple (Matt. 9:9) and was known as a "friend of tax collectors" (Matt. 11:19). Later on he suggested that "tax collectors . . . are entering the kingdom of God ahead of you" (Matt. 21:31).

There is another group of players in the drama of the gospel story that seems to always be against Jesus and for whom Jesus had nothing but rebuke: those in positions of political and social power in Jerusalem. Jesus appears to have seen himself as a prophet to them in particular; he quoted Jeremiah

Yet hints in the Gospels show us that even the relationship between Jews and Romans were not that clear-cut: Luke 7:4–5 suggests that a centurion built the synagogue in Capernaum, the city that Jesus chose as the center of his ministry in Galilee. And some of the earliest non-Jewish believers were Roman and held military office, such as Cornelius, who was a "devout" man who "feared God" (Acts 10:2). That expression, "fear God," goes back at least to Deuteronomy 10:12, but at the end of the Second Temple period it took on a new meaning: Gentiles who respected Judaism, attended synagogue, and kept the commandments as best as they could were called "God-fearers" (see Acts 13:16: "Men of Israel and God-fearers, listen!" Or 13:26: "Men and brothers, sons of Abraham's family, and those of you among us who fear God . . .").

Gustave Doré, *The Sermon on the Mount*, engraving, 1877 (detail).

as he flipped over their tables (Luke 19:46). And although the details are complicated, we can say with reasonable certainty that these are the people who orchestrated his killing and thus were his real enemies – the religious and political elites from the party of the Sadducees who had made alliances with the Roman occupiers.

The synoptic Gospels mention the word "Sanhedrin" in connection with Jesus' trial. The Sanhedrin was an official body of seventy-one members that could adjudicate cases. Yet in these accounts of Jesus' trial it's not clear whether it was the official body of the Sanhedrin that condemned Jesus, or whether it was just a bunch of its members who wanted him dead. For one thing, an assembly of the whole Sanhedrin would require the participation of both Pharisees and Sadducees. Yet if there were Pharisees involved, Matthew, Mark, and Luke do not seem to remember. For another, both Luke and John say nothing about a formal verdict of the Sanhedrin, which is a little odd if it was in fact an official trial. And an assembly of the full Sanhedrin had to happen in the right place, not at the high priest's house during the night, as Matthew and Mark report.

Flusser points out one more detail that in his estimation makes it even more likely that Jesus was not "officially" condemned to death but rather eliminated by people who wanted him dead: it was established as a matter of law that prisoners condemned to capital punishment should be buried in either of the two gravesites in Jerusalem reserved for them (see Mishnah *Sanhedrin* 6:5). Jesus was buried in neither, but in Joseph of Arimathea's new tomb. Joseph was a member of the council. He buried Jesus with the help of Nicodemus, who according to rabbinic sources was one of the three richest men in Jerusalem. They apparently weren't Jesus' enemies, even if Caiaphas and Annas and the others present at his trial were.

While we can't know everything that was going on back then in the upper echelons of political power in Jerusalem, the picture the Jewish historian Josephus paints is pretty dire. For instance, when Valerius Gratus (predecessor to Pontius Pilate) was procurator of Judea, he took it upon himself to appoint the high priests, with no regard for whether they belonged to a priestly family or not. Within less than five years, this Roman governor had set up and deposed five people from the high priesthood (an office traditionally held for life – at least Numbers 35:28 assumes that), ending with Caiaphas (see *Antiquities* 18:32–35). We can only imagine what kind of machinations were going on behind the scenes.

Those in power over us, particularly when they abuse their power for their own interests, are easy to hate – and much harder to love.

When the Gospel writers say "chief priests," they're referring to these Roman puppets without any legitimate claim to the office who were simply there because Rome wanted them there. These people – the people so tightly allied with Roman power that they allowed pagans to dictate who could come into the Holy of Holies on the Day of Atonement – are the sort of unlovable people Jesus loved, and asked his disciples to love.

Now, as I perch high above the Sea of Galilee, feeling the breeze off the lake as Jesus and his listeners must have, I'm left wondering what this means for us today. Who are those whom Jesus wants us to love? Yes, the marginalized, for sure. The outcast. The downtrodden. Those, in a way, are easy to love, because loving them makes us feel like Jesus. But the outcast were not the "enemy." Those in power over us, particularly when they abuse their power for their own interests, are easy to hate – and much harder to love.

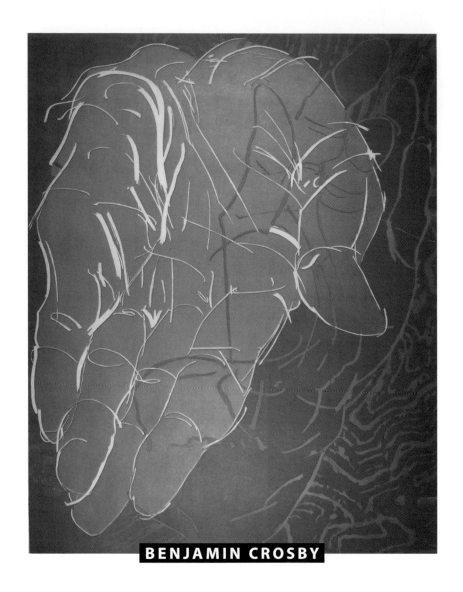

BENJAMIN CROSBY

Foolhardy Wisdom

*Can we love our enemies
in an unforgiving society?*

IN THE WINTER OF 1659, THE DUTCH Anabaptist Dirk Willems made a daring escape from the prison where he was being held by the Roman Catholic authorities because of his faith. According to the *Martyrs Mirror*, a compendium of accounts of the persecution and killing of Anabaptists by both Roman Catholic and magisterial Protestant authorities in early modern Europe, he fled across a frozen pond with a guard in hot pursuit. The guard was evidently heavier than Willems, for while the Anabaptist was able to traverse the pond without difficulty, the ice broke under the guard, and he plunged into the freezing waters. The guard cried out for help, and Willems turned back and helped the man back onto land. As a result, Willems was recaptured; even his saving the guard's life did not win him a reprieve. He was burned at the stake on May 16, 1659, repeatedly crying out, "Oh my Lord, my God!"

What does it mean to love your enemies and to forgive those who wrong you? For the Christian, this question is inescapable. After all, these two related commands to love enemies and forgive wrongdoers are repeated frequently throughout the Gospels. Consider, for example, this famous portion of Jesus' Sermon on the Mount, "You have heard that it was said, 'You shall love your neighbor and hate your enemy.' But I say to you, Love your enemies and pray for those who persecute you, so that you may be children of your Father in heaven" (Matt. 5:43–45). Later, on the way to Jerusalem to meet his death, Jesus teaches his disciples about forgiveness; when Peter asks him how often he should forgive someone sinning against him, offering that he might forgive a wrongdoer a full seven times, Jesus responds, "Not seven times, but, I tell you, seventy-seven times" (Matt. 18:22). He goes on to tell a parable that never fails to convict me (Matt. 18:23–35): Once there was a servant who owed a massive debt to his master but could not pay it. The servant begged for pity and, moved to mercy, the master canceled his entire debt. Then the servant saw another servant who owed him a pittance but, despite his cries for mercy, threw him in prison when he could not pay. When the master heard of this, he threw the first servant into prison until he repaid his entire debt. "So my heavenly Father will also do to every one of you, if you do not forgive your brother or sister from your heart," Jesus concludes (Matt. 18:35). This connection between our own forgiveness and our forgiving others their wrongs against us is so basic that Jesus includes it in the prayer that he taught us to pray: "forgive us our trespasses, as we forgive those who trespass against us." And, of course, Jesus on the cross prays that those who crucified him might be forgiven (Luke 23:34), an example which the deacon Stephen follows while he is being stoned to death (Acts 7:60).

For much of the history of the church, the example of martyrs like Dirk Willems was held up as the ideal of a Christlike relationship to one's enemies: doing good to them even at the cost of one's own life. To be sure, not all theologians would describe behavior like Willems's as morally obligatory in all situations, but this sort of self-sacrificial enemy-love was highly commended.

Benjamin Crosby is a priest in the Episcopal Church serving in the Anglican Church of Canada and a doctoral student in ecclesiastical history at McGill University.

Opposite: Mary Farrell, *Terrain / Offering*, reduction woodcut, 1999.

While this sort of enemy-love has always been countercultural, however, in the last century it has increasingly been criticized by voices from inside the church as well. The Christian teaching that one must love one's enemies and forgive wrongdoers, the critique goes, has been used by oppressors to keep the oppressed down. The oppressed are

---

The Christian teaching that one must love one's enemies and forgive wrongdoers, the critique goes, has been used by oppressors to keep the oppressed down.

---

encouraged to emulate Jesus in embracing undeserved suffering and told that they will be rewarded in eternal life. In the meantime, they are trampled upon by the rich and powerful, who find ingenious ways to excuse themselves from following the ethic of enemy-love they profess. Feminist, black, and womanist theologians have noted in the last fifty years the ways that race and gender impinge upon Christian expectations of forgiveness or norms of enemy-love. They have pointed out that women are often expected to forgive in situations where for a man to forgive would be deemed unmanly, that black people are often called to immediately forgive white oppressors. These thinkers have shown how Christian commitments to self-sacrificial forgiveness and enemy love can lead – indeed, have led – to women being told to remain with abusive partners, to racial minorities being told to passively accept their lot.

It is hard to deny that these critiques have some purchase. Take, for example, the revelations of abuse cover-ups in the Southern Baptist Convention, the way in which predatory pastors were protected by injunctions to forgiveness without

any accountability. Prominent pastors continue to counsel women experiencing emotional and even physical abuse to see such abuse as their cross to bear, and to forgive their husbands without expecting a change of behavior. To borrow a term from the Episcopalian theologian Lauren Winner, we might discuss these troubling applications of Jesus' command to forgive enemies in terms of characteristic damage: the way that, because of the Fall, even good practices given to us by God can go dangerously awry in ways related to the goodness at which these practices aim. But granted that the command to forgive or to love enemies can and does go wrong, and go wrong in ways that often add to the burdens of those most heavily burdened in our society, what are we to do?

ONE ANSWER, increasingly popular among members of the secular and the religious left alike, is to either jettison this talk of enemy-love or redefine it nearly beyond recognition. Some popular feminist writing simply asserts that any expectation or norm of forgiveness is wrong, a tool to deny women their rightful rage against mistreatment. Similarly, public declarations of forgiveness by black people for wrongs committed against them, especially by white people, are often responded to with dismay. Certain sectors of the left reacted negatively to the forgiveness expressed by survivors of the Emmanuel AME Church shooting in 2015, and by the brother of Botham Jean, who was murdered by white police officer Amber Guyger in 2018. In both cases, the victims' families described their offer of forgiveness as stemming from their Christian faith, but critics saw it as a capitulation to cultural scripts underwritten by white supremacy.

For Christians, of course, Jesus' clear and unambiguous commands to forgive and love enemies make it rather difficult to argue against forgiveness altogether. But many justice-minded Christians find themselves redefining it, arguing that what practices of forgiveness or enemy-love are really about is the nonviolent struggle for liberation. One popular reading of the Sermon on the Mount's injunctions to suffer wrongdoing without resistance or revenge asserts – with no backing I can find in the history of Christian exegesis, and no particular plausibility – that, appearances notwithstanding, Jesus' teaching is really about the revolutionary practice of standing up for oneself and forcing one's oppressor to see one's humanity. And so forgiveness becomes a particular sort of self-assertion. Perhaps more popular is asserting that, even if forgiveness is a good idea in theory, it is inappropriate for the church to explicitly call people to love their enemies, especially across boundaries of racial or gender difference. On this argument, it simply isn't for the church to enjoin forgiveness or enemy-love on others, especially others who are part of historically or presently oppressed groups. There may be a universal command to forgiveness, but the church has been so sullied by its past misuse of this command that any church teaching on it is seen as engaging in respectability politics or policing the actions of the marginalized.

Perhaps one of the clearest examples of how this rejection of forgiveness and love of enemies looks in practice can be found on social media. "Cancel culture" is a term too diffuse and imprecise in meaning to be very useful, but it is hard to ignore that progressive-leaning internet circles, Christian or no, tend to be dominated by an attitude of mutual suspicion and uncharitableness. Vicious character attacks are justified as "calling out oppression"; never forgetting a slight (indeed, keeping records via screenshots of tweets or Instagram posts judged problematic) is "holding people accountable"; forgiveness and reconciliation, if they are possible at all, occur only through humiliating rituals of self-abasement. This is something that people on the left are often nervous to talk publicly about

Mary Farrell, *Tension*, etching, 2007.

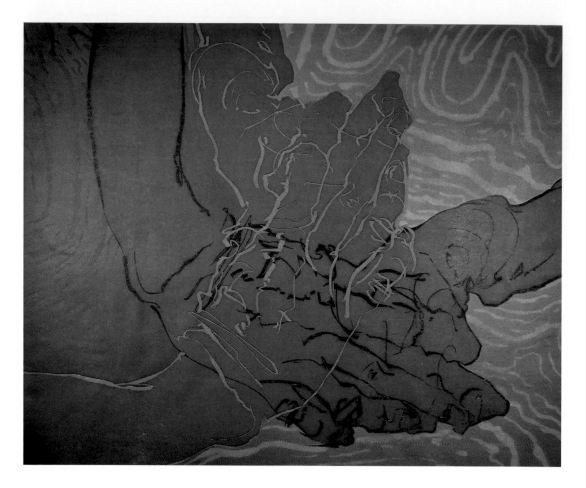

lest they let down the team and give ammunition to conservatives (and open themselves up to character assassination from their erstwhile comrades as punishment). But anyone who has spent a significant amount of time on left-wing social media will know exactly what I mean. While it is undoubtedly true that norms encouraging forgiveness and love of enemies were unevenly applied in the past and continue to be so today, in ways that add to the burden of already burdened people, a world that rejects these norms entirely is an ugly one indeed.

I hasten to add that the rejection of commitments to enemy-love and forgiveness is not only a feature of the contemporary left. As a former union organizer and a mainline Protestant minister, this is the culture that I know best. And frankly, it is the feminist, womanist, and black theology criticisms of the practice of loving your enemies and forgiving those who wrong you that I find most trenchant, even if ultimately unsatisfactory.

Particularly among hyper-online conservatives, a fascination with thinkers like Friedrich Nietzsche and Carl Schmitt have led to a politics that similarly has nothing good to say about forgiveness or loving enemies. Politics – and not infrequently ethics too – are reduced to what Schmitt called the "friend-enemy distinction," in which the goal of one's efforts is not seeking the common good but rewarding friends and punishing (ideally, destroying) enemies. The expectation of forgiveness, especially for so-called victim classes, is seen as evidence of a twisted, life-denying slave morality created by the weak

Mary Farrell, *Confluent Terrain*, reduction woodcut, 2000.

to restrain and control the strong. Sometimes this veers explicitly into the language of racial grievance. Thus, for example, in an inversion of the concern of black radicals mentioned above, among some corners of the right, white Americans who publicly forgive wrongdoers who are black have surrendered to contemporary progressivism's supposed construction of black people as blameless victims. In light of the history of race and racism in the United States, this idea is both hateful and absurd.

The broader point is that on the right as well as the left in the United States, there is a widespread

---

In an increasingly graceless culture, the public witness of Christians as the sort of people who forgive and love even those who have wronged them could be attractive indeed.

---

discomfort with the place of fading Christian norms of forgiveness and love of enemies in our public and private life. For many, Dirk Willems looks less like a heroic example of Christian virtue than a fool or a patsy.

And yet – to put it bluntly – if Dirk Willems is a fool, it's hard to escape the conclusion that the martyrs through the ages all the way back to Jesus Christ himself were fools too. I don't think that we can lay claim to Christianity if we reject some of Jesus' clearest and most unambiguous commands to us. Forgiveness and love of enemies are central enough to our faith that in the prayer that Jesus himself gave us, the prayer that as an Anglican priest bound to the daily office I recite at least five times a day, our own forgiveness is linked to our forgiveness of those who wrong us. To follow Jesus here might be a deep trial – many patristic

commentators on the Sermon on the Mount dwell on just how little we like loving our enemies – and it might indeed be a trial that is unevenly distributed among people. But it is what we are called to do, and how could we fail to obey our good and gracious Savior?

What's more, it seems to me that we have more reasons than just our Lord's example to move us – although that should be more than enough! In an increasingly graceless culture, the public witness of Christians as the sort of people who forgive and love even those who have wronged them could be attractive indeed; speaking from personal experience, communities that refuse to extend grace or forgiveness are incredibly unpleasant to belong to. So how can we hold to Jesus' clear command to forgive and love our enemies while also standing for justice?

CONCERNS THAT CHRISTIAN ETHICS of forgiveness and love of enemies function as a means of further injuring the oppressed would have come as no surprise to Howard Thurman. Early in his magisterial *Jesus and the Disinherited* (1949), he writes,

> I belong to a generation that finds very little that is meaningful or intelligent in the teachings of the Church concerning Jesus Christ. . . . The desperate opposition to Christianity rests in the fact that it seems, in the last analysis, to be a betrayal of the Negro into the hands of his enemies by focusing his attention upon heaven, forgiveness, love, and the like.

Yet Thurman wishes to defend the value of the Christianity of Jesus – if not that of the slave-master – for those "with their backs against the wall," offering a reading of Jesus' teachings as a "technique of survival for the oppressed."

One might expect Thurman to do so by minimizing or ignoring the commands to forgive and to love enemies that bring Christianity into disrepute as useless, if not positively injurious, for those concerned with justice and the remedy of social ills. But Thurman does no such thing. Rather, he addresses hatred as one of the three great ethical temptations of the disinherited, alongside fear and deception, and argues that Jesus' rejection of hatred and command to love enemies and forgive is, perhaps counterintuitively, particularly necessary for those "with their backs against the wall."

This rejection follows upon a careful and not unsympathetic analysis of the way that hatred functions for the disinherited. According to Thurman, simplistic moralizing preaching against hatred fails to understand the psychological role that hatred plays, especially for the disinherited. He suggests that the hatred of one's oppressors often functions as a response to "the estimate that their environment places upon them," namely, that the oppressed somehow deserve their lot. Hatred becomes "a sense of significance which you fling defiantly into the teeth of their estimate of you." In this sense, hatred can serve a vital role in self-realization in the midst of the psychological torment of oppression. Furthermore, it allows the oppressed to use any and all means against their oppressors without "moral disintegration," demarcating a sphere in which "it is open season all the time" – in relation to the hated oppressors – while preserving a sphere in which normal moral rules apply. So, for the oppressed, Thurman thinks, hatred functions to preserve a sense of self and moral integrity.

And yet, unlike some of the contemporary critics of forgiveness and enemy-love, Thurman does not stop there. Hatred may be psychologically productive, but it is nonetheless a "hound of hell" that must be fought against. For despite its seeming benefits, "hatred destroys finally the core of the life of the hater," Thurman believes; it cannot be confined to those whose oppressive behavior initially provokes hatred, but comes to dominate all one's relationships with others. And so "Jesus rejected hatred" – not, Thurman

is careful to note, because he lacked "strength" or "vitality" or even "incentive," but because "he saw that hatred meant death to the mind, death to the spirit, death to communion with his Father." Hatred is ultimately "the great denial" of life; Jesus "affirmed life." Jesus called us, the disinherited included, to love our enemies – not just our personal enemies, not opponents within our in-group, but enemies that are to us as the Romans were to Jesus. As Thurman puts it, "the religion of Jesus says to the disinherited: 'Love your enemy. Take the initiative in seeing ways by which you can have the experience of a common sharing of mutual worth and value. It may be hazardous, but you must do it.'"

T O B E S U R E , this does not mean that discernment need not be exercised in how we love our enemies, that we do not need to decide which hazards need to be embraced and which are better avoided. Forgiveness need not always entail reconciliation; there are people whom – even if we will their good and do not hold their wrongs against them – we may be unable to be in relationship with until Jesus returns to make all things right.

John Calvin offers some advice as to what love of enemies looks like in practice (whether or not he always put this advice into practice is another matter). In Calvin's commentary on the synoptic Gospels, he distinguishes between two forms of forgiveness while addressing Matthew 18. The first form is that, regardless of whether the person repents, the Christian must "lay . . . aside the desire of revenge . . . not cease to love him, but even repay kindness in place of injury." That is, in response to wrongdoing, the Christian must always forgive in the sense of loving the wrong-doer and treating him well. If the wrongdoer repents, then the Christian is to "receive a brother into favor, so as to think favorably respecting him, and to be convinced that the remembrance of his offense is blotted out in the sight of God."

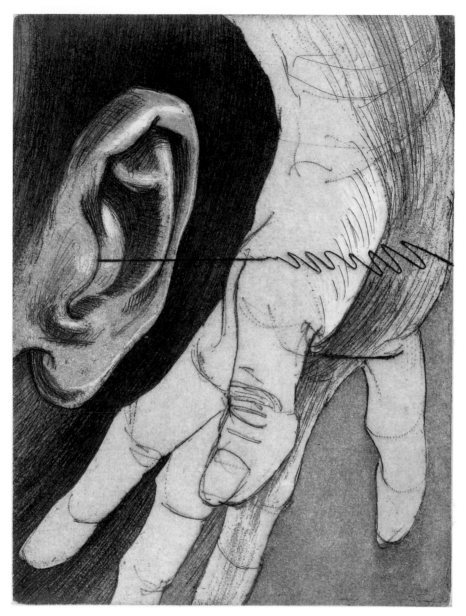

Mary Farrell, *The Challenge of Injustice*, etching, 2007

But here, Calvin adds, "Christ does not deprive believers of the exercise of judgment"; while Christians must indeed always offer the first form of forgiveness and offer the second form of forgiveness freely in response to genuine repentance, we are not obliged to "yield a foolish readiness of belief to every slight expression."

Indeed, in some cases, when someone has wronged us, "we may grant pardon when he asks it, and yet may do so in such a manner as to watch over his conduct for the future, that our forbearance and meekness, which proceed from the Spirit of Christ, may not become the subject of his ridicule." Forgiveness requires exposing ourselves to hazard, requires erring on the side of mercy and forbearance – but it need not require the accepting of insincere apologies or putting up with a pattern of abuse followed by apology followed by additional abuse. Calvin's schema

---

Those motivated by hatred burn out or fall apart. To endure, one must be grounded in a love that seeks to free both oppressed and oppressor.

---

admits the complications of extending forgiveness while nonetheless calling us to "imitate the goodness of our heavenly Father, who meets sinners at a distance to invite them to salvation."

Thus, without denying the possibility of the characteristic damage associated with forgiveness and love of enemies, we can still embrace it as our Lord's clear command, as an opportunity to emulate our God in extending extravagant grace. We can keep Dirk Willems as an example to emulate.

What's more, we need not fear that our capacity to forgive rests only on our own power, but can take heart that God empowers us to do what he commands. In *The Hiding Place*, Corrie ten Boom describes drawing on this divine power when she was confronted with a former SS guard she remembered from Ravensbruck, who was overjoyed to hear his sins had been forgiven. She, who had just been preaching about forgiveness, could not find it in her heart now to forgive, and so she prayed for help.

> As I took his hand the most incredible thing happened. From my shoulder along my arm and through my hand a current seemed to pass from me to him, while into my heart sprang a love for this stranger that almost overwhelmed me.

And so I discovered that it is not on our forgiveness any more than on our goodness that the world's healing hinges, but on [God's]. When he tells us to love our enemies, he gives, along with the command, the love itself.

To compare the sins she had to forgive and the ones many of us are called to forgive might seem frankly ridiculous, but her initial reaction is surely relatable even to those of us who have endured much lesser wrongs than concentration camps. And so we need to ask: Can the love for her enemy that she received be ours as well?

Back in my union-organizing days, I began to worry that my work with the union was malforming me, that suffering mistreatment myself and seeing the mistreatment of others was turning me into an angry, bitter, sour person. I confided this concern to my organizer. Her own relationship with the church and with Christianity was not simple, but her response to me was a sermon in the vein of Howard Thurman: the only way to truly last in the struggle for justice is to be motivated by love, she said, love not just for one's fellow workers but for the bosses as well. Those motivated by hatred burn out or fall apart. To endure, one must be grounded in a love that seeks to free both oppressed and oppressor from a relation that distorts and damages both.

We Christians have a perfect example of this love: while we were his enemies, with no claim upon his love or goodwill, Jesus Christ died for us, that he might make us his own, transforming us from enemies to friends (Rom. 5:10). God gives us both this example and the grace to (imperfectly but really) follow it in our own lives, pouring his love into our hearts through the Holy Spirit so that we can love and serve even our enemies (Rom. 5:5). May we who dare to name ourselves Christ's friends (John 15:15), washed in his blood and filled with the Holy Spirit, follow him in a life full of costly love toward our enemies, loving and forgiving boldly as he loved and forgave us. ⤙

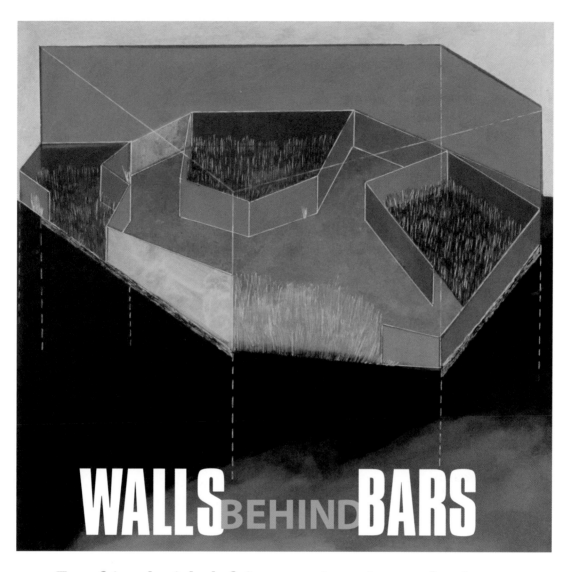

WALLS BEHIND BARS

Two friends risk defying a racist prison subculture.

ANTOINE E. DAVIS and AARON EDWARD OLSON

THE HIGH WALLS of Washington State Penitentiary keep prisoners locked away from the public for a specified period of time, but they don't keep out an evil that has always been a part of public life in the United States.

The vast majority of us who are locked up, no matter what our personal views might be, are forced to participate in a segregated system. Phone use, showers, dining tables, and cells are all separated by race. Groups of prisoners enforce these unwritten rules; officials not only accept but facilitate segregation. Anyone who violates these rules can face sanctions from guards or violence from other prisoners. As a black man (Antoine) and a white man (Aaron), we have each experienced this suffocating pressure.

Aina M. Snape, *Relation Structure*, acrylic on wood, 2014.

Aaron: Forever burned into my memory is a day that I walked the prison's big yard for a breath of fresh air. I watched as another white man finished up his exercise. A group of white prisoners also watched, waiting until he was exhausted from running several miles on the blacktop. Drenched in sweat, he walked slowly, arms in the air, opening his lungs for more oxygen. On cue, an attacker – what prisoners call a "mission boy" – emerged from a huddle of four white convicts sporting shaved heads, swastika tattoos, and small steel hammer necklaces. The designated attacker, barely twenty years old, with fuzz for facial hair, was eighteen months into a twenty-five-year sentence, and it was time to "prove himself" to the senior members of the white supremacists.

The target? Another white supremacist, but one who'd broken the rules by using a shower that belonged to black prisoners. No amount of favor gained in the past could save this young man from the consequences of breaking this cardinal rule. By using a black shower, he had openly disrespected those who enforced the rules and even risked a race riot.

The assault was quick and ruthless. A single sucker punch brought the man to his knees. Five more strikes to the face drove home the point. Blood poured from his nose, mouth, and eyes. Within seconds, the prison guard's bullhorn came blaring from the gun tower, "Stop, stop fighting, get down!" Other guards rushed into the yard screaming the same orders. The mission boy dropped to his knees, lying prostrate, surrendering himself satisfactorily.

On the opposite end of the yard, the white supremacists smirked with approval.

Antoine E. Davis is serving a sixty-three-year prison sentence in Washington State. After graduating from The Urban Ministry Institute, he received his pastoral license at Freedom Church of Seattle. He is the author of Building Blocks Curriculum for Creating Wholeness, *created to help young community members overcome past and present traumas that lead to destructive behaviors.*

Aaron Edward Olson is serving a sentence of fifty-one years to life in Washington State. Imprisoned since age nineteen, he has survived some of the most violent prisons in America, while becoming a writer, speaker, and co-host of the Abolition Christian *podcast. A prolific voice for prison and sentencing reform, Olson is a former special needs mentor, mental health assistant, and current youth violence prevention liaison, service dog trainer, and full-time prison coach.*

Aina M. Snape, *Passage I*, acrylic on paper, 2014.

Antoine: Of course, not all prisoners embrace these racist rules, let alone condone the violence used to enforce them. But we all face pressures to accept racial segregation. Prisoners coordinate their affiliations by skin color, and prison administrations perpetuate this system by assigning prisoners to cells with those of the same race. From the unit supervisor on down, it's common for guards to refer to a "black cell" or a "white cell." If prisoners somehow wind up with a cellmate of another race, most of the time prison officials will make one of them move. Prisoners who push back on such administrative decisions risk being sanctioned with a "refusal to disperse" and sent to solitary confinement. So they usually accept the segregated status quo for the sake of their own safety. Fearful and facing intimidation, many incarcerated individuals refuse to cross those lines.

My initial encounter with this fact came as Diablo, a young Hispanic man, and I shot hoops on the basketball court one day to pass the time. We laughed and conversed about family, just two men talking and enjoying one another's company. I had multiethnic friendships before being incarcerated, as did he, and the two of us were relatively new to the prison system and weren't thinking about racial lines. We simply saw one another as people.

As we continued to laugh and talk, nearly forgetting that we were incarcerated, I tossed the ball to Diablo, but before he could take another shot he was confronted by a Hispanic man. The guy's face was covered with tattoos, with the number 13 on his neck in Old English lettering, a mark of the Sureños gang. Off to the side, a group of Hispanic prisoners was watching him from a distance, their appearance and behavior suggesting gang affiliation.

After the man whispered into his ear, Diablo's smile vanished, as if he had been stripped of something valuable. When the stranger passed me, he gazed at me with an arrogant expression of triumph. Diablo hung his head, reluctantly letting the ball slip from his hands. As the ball bounced and rolled toward the fence coiled with razor wire, I asked, "Hey man, where you going?" With fear in his eyes and voice, he responded, "I can't play with you," drifting over to the group of Hispanic prisoners who had just defined the parameters of his life.

The physical threat to anyone who fails to comply with the rules of segregation had extinguished our connection. The pressures to conform overrode our nascent friendship, encouraging him to regard me as an enemy because of my skin color.

Aaron: There's a famous adage: "When you're going through hell, keep going." It was March 20, 2013, and I sat in my cell waiting for the guard to announce that it was time for recreation. The small speaker crackled, and a faint voice came over the intercom. "Olson?" came the soft call, a noticeable change from the usual commands barked at us. "Yeah?" I replied. "The CUS wants to see you in her office, please." The intercom went silent.

An unscheduled beckoning to the correctional unit supervisor's office is rarely a good thing, and the anxiety started. I put my shoes on and straightened my khaki top and bottom. My counselor and the CUS met me in the hallway. With grim faces, they locked eyes on me. I wondered if I was being taken to solitary confinement, fearing another long stint of isolation but masking my angst.

"It's your mom," said the CUS. I could guess what was coming, but I pretended not to understand, with a lump in my throat. "She passed away."

"What?" I said, confused. "How?" I searched her eyes, empathetic for the first time in the nine months I had known her. The woman with ice in her veins mustered compassion for the moment. "I think your mom committed suicide."

I was paralyzed. I would rather have gotten solitary confinement than this horrifying news. She added, "I think she shot herself. That's what your sister said." Images of my mom shooting herself immediately overwhelmed me, and I felt confined to a prison within a prison, tormented and helpless to do anything for my loved ones.

"Can I make a phone call?" I asked. "Sure," she replied. I called my sister-in-law, Anela. She answered the phone in tears, explaining that my mother had shot herself two days prior.

I went into "hope mode," encouraging Anela and my siblings to have faith that we would make it through this. I agreed to write a eulogy, "A Mother by Trade." I attribute my strength in that particular moment to my relationship with God. When I was hopeless, hope is what he gave me.

To truly support our friend in a segregated culture, we would be forced to weave our way through racism and hate.

In turn, I was able to pour hope into my family, knowing that we were in the midst of what felt like a hopeless situation. I was thankful that I was able to comfort those I love. But when I hung up the phone, I wondered who would comfort me.

In prison, news spreads faster than gossip at a Rotary club. The white supremacist shot caller (the leader of a group) came to my cell that evening. "You good?" he asked through the crack in the steel door. I nodded my head, even though I wasn't. I knew he didn't care about me. It was only the second time he had ever spoken to me. He soon revealed the reason for his presence.

"I need you to handle your old celly," he continued. "He's saying he's Caucasian now, and not a white boy." I knew enough to know that my old cellmate's public announcement that he was Caucasian was his way to disassociate himself from the white supremacists. It was also a sure way to a violent exit from general population. The whites wanted to hurt him badly, and I was chosen to carry out the task. Without hesitation, I declined the demand, citing the death of my

mother. The shot caller acted like he'd just heard for the first time, feigning empathy. He departed quickly to continue his search for someone to carry out his order.

During the following two months not one man who aligned with the "whites" asked me if I was OK, or seemed to care about my loss. Instead, my comfort and brotherhood came from an unlikely source. Only seconds after the solicitation from the white supremacist, the intercom crackled again. "Some people want to talk to you," it said. The intercom went silent, and the steel door began to slide open. I could see two black men standing in the large space that divides the two sides of the unit. One of them was Antoine.

Antoine: When I heard that Aaron's mother had committed suicide, I was stricken by grief, trying to imagine what I would feel if I was in his shoes. The emotional rollercoaster left a knot the size of a boulder in my stomach. I wanted to comfort him but wondered what I could say or do under such crushing circumstances.

After another friend and I received permission from one of the guards to speak with Aaron, we went over and prayed with him. After turning to walk away, I could feel the internal tug to do more than just pray. To truly support him in a segregated culture, we would be forced to weave our way through racism and hate, exposing ourselves to the possibility of violence, a reality I was far too familiar with.

The following days, Aaron and I walked, talked, and at times cried together. On multiple occasions we were approached by white prisoners, suggesting we cease all interactions, sometimes with threats. We knew from experience that these threats were serious.

The black prisoners, on the other hand, spoke to me more privately about my frequent interaction with Aaron. After explaining the reason behind my decision to support him, they let me be, saying that I had shown consistency in my claim to be a Christian. Some of the black prisoners made insulting comments, which I expected, but none threatened me, though I could never be too sure that I was safe.

But in spite of the danger, I couldn't abandon a person in need on the basis of his skin color. Yes, it would have been safer to accept the prison norms. But choosing physical safety would have weighed on my conscience, and I couldn't forget Aaron.

Before things came to a boiling point, Aaron was sent out to attend his mother's funeral. Dressed in an orange jumpsuit and shackled with steel cuffs, he was transported by two guards to the one-hour service. When it was over, a case manager informed him that his application for a hardship transfer had been accepted – Aaron was being sent to Washington Corrections Center in Shelton. It was nice to know his hardship would bring him closer to home. Yet it was difficult to swallow the irony that getting closer to his mother, who was no longer alive, was the reason he had applied for the transfer.

Despite the circumstances, I was glad to see him leave the hell known as Washington State Penitentiary. In comparison to other prisons, WSP is a wet blanket that smothers any spark of hope.

With Aaron gone, I still used every opportunity to challenge the ignorance and hatred. I worked on removing racial barriers by plucking one brick from the wall at a time.

After spending a decade of my life in Washington State Penitentiary, I was finally transferred to Shelton, where I was reunited with Aaron.

Aaron and Antoine: While our friendship had a happy outcome, we are more troubled than ever about persistent prison racism, which hurts everyone. Safety, communication, and relationships for all prisoners suffer because of the segregated culture. Not all prisoners like it, but the threat of violence and sanctions hang over anyone who violates these rules. Even worse, the Department of Corrections, which claims to protect safety and rehabilitate prisoners, endorses racist behavior by dividing the population into black, white, and Hispanic cells and allowing other unwritten prohibitions to go unquestioned. This not only deepens racism in prison but reinforces that way of living as the norm once prisoners return home.

Our hope is that one day the leadership in the Department of Corrections will care enough to change the brutal culture within its facilities. An opportunity to challenge the larger culture's racism is being ignored, making life more dangerous and reinforcing ideas that have destructive consequences inside or outside prison. ⤳

Aina M. Snape, *Structure III,* acrylic on wood, 2014.

Students Brave the Heat

Conflict can be fruitful when students don't just debate, but listen to one another.

LEAH LIBRESCO SARGEANT

A GOOD ENMITY looks like this – a circle of chairs under the pallid flicker of fluorescent classroom lights. I worked with the University of North Carolina–Chapel Hill Agora fellows to set up a tight ring initially. If attendance was low, they could still gather closely, with their classmates – their opponents – close enough to touch. But as the door swung open again and again, the circle kept pulsing outward. Spaces were filled, seats scooted back, new chairs were pulled off the stack to fill the gaps.

By the time I pulled my gavel out of my purse and handed off my baby to the sitter, we had a little over forty students ready to try to fight

about abortion one more time, but this time, to fight *better*.

My colleagues and I crisscross the country holding debates on college campuses as part of the Braver Angels Debates and Discourse program. This is our pitch: a space for fruitful conflict, with an equal emphasis on both words. I'm proud of the work we do, but much of the credit belongs to our participants. Plato conceived the role of the teacher as helping students recollect what they already possess, and I think our debates work the same way. We offer a venue where students bring the best of themselves – I'm a midwife, not a ringmaster.

Sometimes, programs centered on dialogue are skittish about allowing sharp disagreement. Their hesitation reinforces to participants that open acknowledgement of conflict is too dangerous to attempt. Debate puts the conflict front and center, so no one needs to worry about making a "mistake" by sparking a real disagreement.

Our format is intended to make that conflict fruitful by offering a transparently fair process. We call on timed speeches, each side getting equal turns. There is no division between speakers and watchers – anyone can participate by speaking or asking a question, and even attendees who do not speak know they have as much access to the floor

Leah Libresco Sargeant's writing has appeared in the New York Times, First Things, *and* FiveThirtyEight. *She runs the Substack* Other Feminisms, *and is the chief of staff for Braver Angels's Debates and Public Discourse program.*

as anyone else. Everyone is heard, and everyone has to answer questions in good faith.

The debates require attendees to adopt a heightened tone – speakers address each other by surname; people posing questions must rise to ask them; and, finally, questions are directed to the chair, rather than at the speaker. In practice this means that it is forbidden to ask, "How could you say some lives aren't worth living? Have you ever *met* the people you're talking about?" but permissible to say, "Madame Chair, I wonder whether the gentleman thinks that informed consent to an abortion on the basis of disability would require the parents to meet people living with that disability?" This indirect way of asking questions allows speakers to hear clearly that their ideas are being examined, rather than their selves being attacked.

It's tricky to strike the right balance. Questioners may be motivated by a just anger, and we want to leave room for *parrhesia* – challenging, prophetic speech. But the goal of asking a question is to receive an answer. We want a hard question to be a gift to the speaker, an invitation to set aside self-protection for the sake of the truth.

With each of these rules, we try to make the debate space different from all the prior spaces where one may have fought about this topic. I often start events by asking people to raise their hand if they've had a bad conversation on our given topic recently, and then point out that those who raised their hand came to the event motivated by trust and hope – hope that a better conversation is possible, and trust that other people are seeking that too.

In my opening spiel on the rules and their purpose, I always tell the debaters that I can't guarantee things will go well, but, if nothing else, I want them to go wrong *differently* than they have before. The debate is meant to be an escape route from the current conversational ruts.

THE ARGUMENT at UNC began long before I arrived on campus. Each of our debates is framed around a specific resolution, and drafting them is tougher than it seems. It's the part of our formal debate process that tends to get the most pushback. People who are divided from each other know what topic they're debating, and they often feel like it should be as simple as saying "Gun Control: Yes or No?" "Abortion: Yes or No?" But often, it's the process of choosing a resolution that begins to reveal how little we know the people who oppose us.

The group organizing the debate tilted prochoice, so if they wanted to debate the morality of abortion, they would have to recruit pro-life speakers from elsewhere on campus – speakers who were a little reluctant to "out" themselves at a liberal-leaning school. The Agora fellows began by borrowing from the language of political talking points, proposing "Resolved: The government should define life to begin at conception" or "Resolved: Abortion should be illegal after twenty weeks with exceptions for rape, incest, and medical emergencies."

The problem with framing a debate around the possible political compromise of twenty weeks was that it didn't map well onto what either side wanted. A debate works best when it's aimed at the heart of what divides the opposing sides. In politics, one might settle for an uncomfortable compromise, but, in the debate, we want students to be able to make the case for what they actually believe. The goal is to offer one's position as an invitation, an open door for one's enemy to walk through.

Since the group was struggling to get pro-lifers on their planning committee, we pivoted to consider resolutions that would help speakers explore conflicting values within a pro-choice-leaning group. After some discussion, the group settled on "Resolved: Abortion is justifiable on the basis of expected disability."

The first speakers were arranged in advance, but there seemed to be one speech made in silence, before the debate formally began. As the chairs were scraped across the floor and rearranged, there was suddenly a still point in the general scuffle. A blind student had entered, one hand on his cane, the other on a classmate's arm. We cleared a space for him near a gap in the ring, and one student crossed the room to check if he needed anything. Was it helpful to offer a verbal description of the space in which, shortly, we would debate whether his parents should have been able to judge whether it was a mistake to let him occupy space at all?

The first speaker took the floor, glancing briefly at the blind student, and then launched into his planned remarks. He intended to make a case to his fellow pro-choice students as a simple matter of logic. If they, like he, endorsed the slogan

"Abortion on demand, and without apology," how could they object to abortions on the basis of anticipated disability?

The goal of asking a question is to receive an answer. A hard question is a gift, an invitation to set aside self-protection for the sake of the truth.

Imagine, he said, a woman is going to a clinic for an abortion. Everyone who is pro-choice supports her right to make that choice and also holds that she is the only one who can judge if that choice is right. His fellow pro-choicers think it would be an injustice if someone cross-examined her or asked her to justify her abortion before the procedure. Now, he said, suppose she volunteers the reason, and says the abortion is because of anticipated disability.

"How could you flip your position on her abortion upon learning that?" he asked. Especially if you thought women should be able to have abortions simply because they had a right to not be pregnant against

their will, how could learning one fact about *this* fetus have a bearing on that right? Did pro-choice speakers in the negative of the resolution really want to argue that women only had a right to abort completely healthy babies?

It was an excellent opening speech. It's tempting, both on and off the debate floor, to try to box your enemy in with a flurry of arguments. Debaters who are playing to an audience often use the strategy known as the "Gish gallop" where they raise enough arguments quickly enough that it's impossible for their opponent to refute them all. What this speaker did was the opposite. He raised one argument, going slowly enough that he could explain why he saw it as pivotal.

As the chair, I had the chance to ask questions myself, and so I embroidered a little on his scenario. Picture the doctor in the procedure room, someone who has built her life around guaranteeing abortion access, someone perfectly willing to perform an abortion in the abstract. She lays out her curette blades, picks up the speculum, and then the woman on the table says, "Thank you, we *absolutely* didn't want a girl." Is the abortion doctor a hypocrite if she puts down her tools and refuses to carry out the abortion?

The speaker paused, genuinely considering the question. In a good debate, the answers often come haltingly, as speakers are jostled a little from what they've gone over in their head again and again, and into a bit of ground they haven't explored. He told me that he hadn't thought as much about conscience objections in the context of this debate, but he'd have sympathy for a doctor who didn't want to perform abortions on the basis of sex, particularly if the parents weren't just trying to balance their family, but had a clear

sense of girls as "less-than." Ultimately, though, he thought that *someone* should be willing to carry out the procedure – after all, what kind of life potentially awaited the child in a family that didn't want her?

Speakers on both sides of the resolution kept turning over his example, expanding it, altering it, trying to see how their own moral intuitions

---

In a good debate, the answers often come haltingly, as speakers are jostled a little from what they've gone over in their head again and again, and into a bit of ground they haven't explored.

---

handled his question. It's the personal rejection that was the problem for one student. The whole question of abortion on the basis of disability, she said, presumed that "parents are OK with *a* child, but not *this* child – that's what makes it discrimination."

The speeches in our debate alternated affirmative and negative, without any further attempt to coordinate on each side. Each speech was too short to cover everything, so speakers focused on a particular facet of the discussion, building up a fuller picture of where and why they differed in the same way that an ultrasound offers blurry, flattened glimpses of the child veiled by the womb.

Flicker-flick: a bright ulna amid shadows, *blur-focus:* the parents look at the sharp profile and nose, the technician notes the nuchal fold thickness with dismay. *Fuzz-resolve:* is that a hole in the argument? Is that a hole in the heart?

As the debate went on, the speeches started to revolve around a new question – how clearly could they differentiate between curing a disability and killing the disabled? If a parent faced a threefold choice – to receive the child as is, to intervene in utero and somehow resolve the medical difference, to abort this child and try again – how could the students articulate which choice(s) were permissible?

Down syndrome and Deafness were the examples the students began circling. Can you have a culture that takes pride in a particular difference if it is possible and encouraged to cure it? Does that imply the community around the difference was always a coping mechanism, which should be superseded by a real cure? With a wide gap between how people imagine they'd feel living with a disability versus how disabled people self-report, what does it mean for parents to offer informed consent on behalf of their child?

One student argued that the *decision* might be hard, but the question of the *decider* was not. "The mother is the only one who can speak to the interest of the child," he said. "Only the mother?" one questioner asked, and the speaker admitted he didn't quite know how to fit in the father. Other students kept prodding at who could speak for the child's interest – can a Deaf community claim that, by virtue of their shared Deafness, they better know the child's needs than the child's parents?

As the students left off speaking about "disability" in the abstract and began debating which specific differences made life not worth living, I noticed more of them glancing at the blind student. One student tried to draw a clearer dividing line between the people present in the room and the implications of the resolution by focusing on *whether* there is a person in the womb. He asked one speaker in the negative whether she could be making a mistake in extrapolating backward from how we treat disabled adults and children to how we treat fetuses with disability markers. Wasn't it possible she was extrapolating out of the realm where it was possible to "discriminate" since discrimination presumed choosing among *persons*?

At last a student rose, in the affirmative, for whom the questions we'd been batting about were not abstract. It wasn't the student with the visible disability, but a quiet boy who hadn't stood out to me. He spoke of how his family had immigrated to the United States from Saudi Arabia. When his mother next conceived, their finances were shaky. Sickle cell disease ran in his family, and prenatal testing revealed the baby had the trait. In sickle cell disease, blood cells are malformed. Instead of smooth, dimpled disks, they form sickle shapes that can interlock and clot, causing severe, chronic pain and other complications. Sickle cell disease can be treated with drugs and blood transfusions, but it requires vigilance and reliable access to affordable care. For this new immigrant family, it was the uncertainty about

whether they could care for their child that led them to choose abortion. His parents hadn't kept the choice secret from their other children, and he thought they had made the right decision.

A few years later, when they were better established, his mom conceived again, and this time,

---

The students realize that anyone in the room might be the living embodiment of the hypothetical they are batting around.

---

prenatal testing revealed that the baby had Down syndrome. His parents happily chose to carry their child to term, more confident they were now able to meet a medically complex child's needs.

After he spoke and answered questions, the students had a sharper sense that anyone in the room might be the living embodiment of the hypothetical they were batting around. It was then that the blind student rose to speak. He felt many speakers had been too confident that they could assess what disability felt like from the inside. He brought up disability writer Eva Feder Kittay's distinction between seeking *the* good life versus *a* good life. His life is different from a sighted person's, but it is possible to find a good life. And the narrowness that might cause opposing speakers to miss what "good"

could mean in the context of difference and disability might also limit what their own good life could look like.

AT THE END OF THE DEBATE, we broke off from the heightened, adversarial format, and held a final debriefing discussion, asking participants to reflect on what they learned and what surprised them. The blind student and the Saudi Arabian student were frequently cited by their classmates for their generosity and trust in laying out their lives before the room, so that people could test their ideas against lived reality. It was more dangerous than abstraction, but it also kept them honest.

Students lingered, chatting with each other, asking more casual follow-up questions about what they'd heard. I had one question of my own. I walked over to the student who had framed his whole speech around evaluating the worth of a life through a utilitarian calculus of Quality Adjusted Life Years. He'd glanced a couple times at written notes, which I couldn't help but notice he'd been taking with his paper braced against Aristotle's *Nichomachean Ethics* for support.

He was clearly a noted and somewhat affectionately received campus provocateur. He'd come out swinging on the floor, in favor both of abortion in the cases of some disability, but also of "curing" some differences, like autism and Deafness, if it was clear enough (as he felt it was) that those differences led to worse quality of life. This had sparked a question about whether he'd submit to a similar cure, if one were found for his cheerful belligerence.

Did the book buzz in protest, I asked him, when you used a treatise on virtue ethics to write down such bluntly consequentialist points? He laughed, and pulled it out from his bag. "I borrowed this from my anti-vax, environmentalist friend!" As he and his classmates streamed out, they carried less visible signs of cross-pollination and gifts received from ostensible enemies. ➤

Photograph by Noel Reynolds. Used by permission.

Lammergeier

Riding a thermal ever higher
With its clutched prize, the lammergeier

Forgets the blood sports of the plain
And banks to swoop again, again

Towards one chosen spot. Released,
The femur of a wildebeest,

Bare bone, no flesh or sinew, plummets
Some thirty feet to a cliff summit's

Rock ledge, whacks it and bounces back
And somersaults but does not crack,

Turns cartwheels threatening to kiss
The sheer brink of the precipice,

And gradually comes to rest,
Unshatterable. Too possessed

By purpose to grow bored or tire,
Time after time the lammergeier

Retrieves the hunk of limb and flies
Aloft to repeat the exercise.

At last the perfect placement strikes
The thigh-bone into shards and spikes,

Sharp delicacies to excite
That strange and perilous appetite.

With the sickening precision seen
In a sword-swallower's routine,

It juggles and contrives to get
A gizzard-skewering bayonet

Of bone into its gaping beak
And gulp, with aeons of technique,

The full length, inch by gruesome inch,
Down its gullet, and does not flinch.

There hardly seems the room to slide
That stomach-puncturing blade inside

Its body. It does not slump or stagger.
Then picks out one more jagged dagger.

STEPHEN EDGAR

Photograph: Noel Reynolds,
Lammergeier (Gypaetus barbatus), 2008.

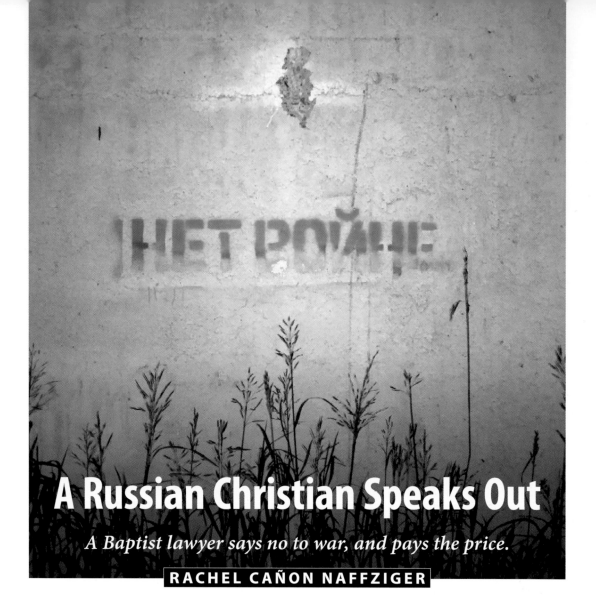

A Russian Christian Speaks Out

A Baptist lawyer says no to war, and pays the price.

RACHEL CAÑON NAFFZIGER

LAST FALL, Egor Redin was in hiding at a Baptist church in Tajikistan, two thousand miles from home. The pastor advised him not to leave the building because the secret police might be watching. Redin had hoped to apply for asylum in Tajikistan but was warned not to. If Tajik authorities found out he was Baptist, he would likely be deported back to Russia, where he would face criminal prosecution for protesting Russia's invasion of Ukraine.

Redin had fled to Tajikistan to avoid Putin's "partial mobilization" of Russians to fight in Ukraine. In his words, "the original plan was to wait out this madness in Tajikistan." As a father of two little girls aged two and four who was also a pacifist (historically Russian Baptists have refused to serve in military positions where they would be required to kill) he should never have had to worry about conscription – religious objectors and fathers of two or more had been exempt

---

Rachel Cañon Naffziger is a nonprofit worker, writer, artist, and a Ukrainian-Argentine American. She lives with her husband and their son on the north side of Chicago.

under Russian law. But that fall he began to hear of other Baptists being sent to prison for refusing the draft. So, on September 24, he packed a small bag with his laptop, a toothbrush and toothpaste, important documents, and a change of socks, and left his homeland, not knowing when he would return. "This" he recalled later, "is what running to save your life looks like."

Shortly after the invasion began, in February 2022, Redin had reposted on Instagram an open letter issued by a nonprofit for which he served as vice president of legal affairs, calling for an end to "this senseless war." A senior television producer in state media who had helped him advance in his career contacted him to warn that his future public and professional life would be greatly complicated by his open opposition to the war. Not long after that, the Russian government made it illegal to even call the war a war. Protesting could mean a prison sentence of up to fifteen years.

Redin hoped he had evaded detection, but after he had fled the country the authorities finally followed up on his antiwar Instagram posts. He felt powerless to protect his wife and children back home. "I made the only decision I could," he told me later, "to flee with my family to the United States."

Following advice from other Russian asylum seekers in Telegram chat groups, Redin determined a route – his family would reunite in Istanbul, Turkey, and fly from there to Cancún, Mexico; then they would travel north to the border and ask for asylum at a point of entry between Tijuana and San Diego.

Redin met his wife and children in Istanbul. While there he planned to peacefully picket the Russian Embassy with a sign saying "no to war," but he was told he would be arrested and deported back to Russia if he did so. Russia and Turkey, he discovered, have had an extradition agreement since 2014. He didn't leave the hotel again until it was time to go to the airport.

Arriving in Mexico, they found a group of Californian Christians who were willing to pay for them to stay at a hotel about a hundred miles south of Tijuana. Redin knew asylum seekers are routinely turned back, so he sought help from an organization called Most V USA (Russian for "Bridge to USA") that promised to get Ukrainian and Russian asylum seekers on a special list with US border officials – for $2,000 per person. Not long after he made an appointment with Most V USA, workers from the organization were arrested in Tijuana while attempting to transport more than $500,000, which they had collected from

Antiwar graffiti from around Russia since the February 2022 invasion of Ukraine; the text нет войне translates as "No to war."

asylum seekers, across the border. The organization canceled all future appointments, including the Redin family's. Initially they were devastated, but in January their prayers were answered: US Customs and Border Protection began allowing asylum seekers to reserve an appointment directly (previously, only nongovernmental organizations or lawyers could request appointments). The Redins quickly claimed asylum and crossed the border uneventfully in early January.

HAD EGOR REDIN not fled Russia, he would likely have become the second in his family to be imprisoned by the state. His grandfather, a Russian Baptist pastor, was sent to the gulag for five years in the 1980s for distributing illegal (Christian) literature.

Baptists have a long history of being persecuted in Russia, though many hoped that had come to an end with the fall of the Soviet Union. The Russian Orthodox Church also initially faced persecution under communism, but eventually Soviet authorities determined that getting Russians to abandon faith was futile. In 1943, Stalin chose to revive the Russian Orthodox Church to spiritually justify annexation of historically Orthodox countries, according to historian Kathryn David. The state and the state-sanctioned church have had a close relationship ever since. Patriarch Kirill, the current head of the Russian Orthodox Church, has called the invasion of Ukraine "a holy war" and declared any Russian soldier who dies in the fight a martyr.

The Russian Orthodox Church is not entirely united behind Kirill: over 150 priests signed a letter protesting the war in March 2022, calling for "reconciliation and an immediate ceasefire." But at the highest level, the church is wedded to political power. One prominent Orthodox television channel owner went so far as to say that Putin was sent by God.

Some Protestant Christian groups, on the other hand, have been labeled anti-government extremists. After Russia's annexation of parts of eastern Ukraine in 2014, the Ukrainian Baptist Union was designated a terrorist group, the Baptist hymnal was banned from the region, and Donetsk Christian University, where several members of Redin's church studied, was destroyed outright. In Russia, new "anti-extremism" legislation was passed in 2016. "Extremism" was vaguely defined, providing a context to imprison pastors and tear down houses used as unregistered churches.

Redin is no extremist; in fact, he had never directly criticized the Russian government before. As a lawyer and campaigner, he had faith in the legal system and worked to reform Russian law and promote the welfare of the orphans his church supported. He was known for taking on cases pro bono and commenting on issues through the media and public speaking. But when Russia invaded Ukraine in February 2022, in violation of international law, Redin sensed he soon wouldn't

Egor Redin with his wife and daughters just after crossing the border into San Diego, January 2023.

be able to count on the protection of Russian law either. "The moment this attack happened, I realized that gradually the laws would stop working and we would become defenseless." And so he began to publicly express his disagreement with the war.

Russian Protestant churches and leaders mostly remained silent in the beginning, or said they were praying about the "situation" in Ukraine – to call it anything else posed a risk not only to them but also to their churches. Then a prominent Ukrainian Baptist leader wrote a letter calling on them to condemn the war without mincing words,

---

Resistance can take many forms, and Russian dissidents have had quite a lot of practice.

---

and in response, over four hundred Russian Protestant leaders called for an end to the war in an open letter, telling fellow Russians: "We need to repent for what we have done, first to God and then to the people of Ukraine. We need to reject lies and hatred. We call on the authorities of our country to stop this senseless bloodshed." Days later, all speech against the war was made illegal.

It's easy to sympathize with those who don't speak out. According to Redin, his church is generally unified in opposition to the war, but most of them, like many Russians, have determined that public protest is futile. A Russian participant in a Carnegie Endowment study mused: "I went to a rally, and what happened? Did it change anything? Yes it did: I was fired!" It's far from clear that public protest is always the right course of action. For one, imprisoned Russians can't directly help vulnerable Russians or Ukrainians. If all the members of Redin's church were imprisoned, the transition home they run

for orphans would cease to exist. And Russian dissidents play a significant role in supporting the estimated 2.85 million Ukrainian refugees in Russia. Resistance can take many forms, and Russian dissidents have had quite a lot of practice.

EGOR REDIN HAS FOUND a Russian Baptist community in the Seattle area, where he and his family have settled as they await their asylum hearings. He is surprised by the level of religious freedom in the United States. In Russia, pastors have to watch what they say in the pulpit; here, the idea that security services would eavesdrop on sermons seems unthinkable. Even nature seems less afraid here, he says: he's seen more wild animals than he ever did in Russia. And he is deeply grateful for the "incredible amount of mutual assistance" in his church, and the support of state social services of Washington State. He thanks God for the opportunity to start a new life in a democratic country.

He also isn't blind to the problems of his new home: he is troubled by the number of unhoused people he sees and wants to help. For now, though, he is focused on helping others who, like him, are seeking asylum from persecution abroad. Recently, he helped start a program through his church to match asylum seekers with guarantors. Guarantors agree to provide an address for important documents to go to and to help asylum seekers adjust to life in the United States. Having a guarantor can help asylum seekers avoid extended detention or immediate deportation, since immigration authorities want to be able to find them easily. Egor recently received his work permit and plans to begin practicing as a lawyer as soon as he can pass an American bar exam, so that he can help others seeking asylum. At present, he does what he can: he publishes information about seeking asylum via a Telegram channel of his own in the United States. ⤙

SARAH CLARKSON

My Mind, My Enemy

When mental illness struck, my mind became my enemy.
Would I battle it, or learn to love it?

WHEN I WAS A CHILD my mind was a gift. Not the practical sort you're supposed to use diligently but the magical kind, the sort of gift you'd find in the hands of your fairy godmother. My imagination was my secret companion. She was mighty and she was wild, and my first memories shimmer and burn with the beauty she revealed. The ordinary scenes of my outdoorsy, bookish childhood became the stuff of high fantasy. She made dryads of my backyard trees, filled the sky with talking stars, and made a heroine of sunburned little me on the commonest of days. I might return from an afternoon at play with the wistful air of an orphan or the lofty brow of a princess in search of her lost throne.

As I grew older, the scenes in my mind spilled into words that I began to scrawl into half-baked poetry and tentative stories about kindly unicorns, then adventure tales, then yearning, windswept epics. As I stood at the cusp of adulthood, I found that my imagination led me into wide, starlit spaces within my own heart, where I lay hushed and wakeful in the long evenings, reaching toward a mystery I desired with all my being.

She brought me so much goodness, until the day she betrayed me.

I was seventeen when my mind became my enemy. I still find it hard to describe the experience of mental illness, of having a psyche you cannot control. From one day to the next, I found that this friend of my childhood bombarded me with almost uninterrupted images of explicit violence, sexual perversion, and disaster. The images were vicious; I could not look at someone I loved without seeing him or her entangled in a horror scene. What I saw was so real, evoking such a physical reaction of panic and such a pervasive sense of shame that I became almost

I took all the frayed faith of my childhood I could grasp and asked God to subdue, or change, or obliterate the broken part of my mind.

unable to cope with normal life. I barely slept. I withdrew from my plans for college. My sense of self disintegrated. My health broke. My mind, this most intimate of companions, had become my enemy, and she was formidable.

It took several months, quite a few counselors, and one psychiatrist to give me a diagnosis of OCD (obsessive-compulsive disorder). The longer-term work of learning to contain and cope with my illness had just begun, but one of the first things ground into me by each professional was

Sarah Clarkson is a writer and author exploring the intersection of good books, beauty, and theology. Her most recent book is This Beautiful Truth: How God's Goodness Breaks into Our Darkness. *She lives in an old Oxford vicarage with her husband Thomas and their three children.*

Photography by Andrey Metelev.

that the horror film in my mind wasn't my fault. This was, on the one hand, a watershed realization for me. To know that I hadn't chosen to fill my mind with violence and twisted sexuality, to know that my breaking wasn't my fault, was to turn from mental disintegration toward sanity.

But it also meant that a central aspect of my coping mechanism was to treat my mind as my enemy. I was taught to interact with my mind in terms of hostility: as something I must resist, fight, subdue. This was a battle and my mind was my foe. My prayers reflected this. I took all the frayed faith of my childhood I could grasp and asked God to subdue, or change, or obliterate

---

I barely recognized myself when I emerged, raw and afraid, from the first months of my illness and began the long-term work of coping with my kind of insanity.

---

the broken part of my mind. This idea was encouraged in me by Christian counselors who linked my illness to demonic influence, and by psychiatrists who told me that medication would subdue the beast within me. The subtext to every formal conversation regarding my illness was the assumption that the right combination of medication and therapy could control my unruly psyche. Because, in the parlance of those specialized worlds, my fractured, rebellious mind was my enemy, something to be beaten into submission.

WHAT DOES IT MEAN to love your enemy? I didn't think of Christ's command in the early days of my illness. I never thought it might apply to my rogue mind, or my frail, maddening self. In fact, I had never considered these words of Jesus except in the abstract.

Loving my sick mind was also unimaginable to me because the enemy language I learned to describe my mind fit quite closely with the language of spiritual combat I heard so often in church settings. I heard suffering described as a foe to be overcome, defeated. Sometimes I felt I was just doing something wrong; if I could just pray the right prayer, or enact the correct number of spiritual disciplines, or exist (somehow) more victoriously, then my illness would retreat like a vanquished army in the face of a greater power.

That's what all the language of conflict and combat centered upon: power. I suppose it makes sense. The promise of God's power at work in our lives is central to the gospel, and we want to see it firsthand: opponents smashed, illness zapped, prosperous lives, and conversions by the thousands. And if our troubles are not obliterated – if we are not changed into powerful people ourselves – we wonder if God has turned against us.

Humans have often been pretty confused about what divine power looks like, but I think we struggle particularly in the modern world to conceive of God's power as anything other than force, because we live in a world of dominative power. We have the relentless mechanical power of technology and the oracular power of unprecedented information and the social power of instant access to mobilize great mobs of people. But these sorts of power are all fundamentally about increased control over ourselves and the world, a kind of power rooted far more in the philosophy of writers like Nietzsche than in the teaching of Christ. Nietzsche understood the "will to power" as the basic drive of human identity, the kind of power that pushes for self-expression, destroying any obstacle in its way. It's easy to baptize this view of power and see God as the ultimate strongman, just waiting to crush all the things we most dislike (including what is weak in ourselves).

But the power of God is Jesus, the suffering servant, born simply to die for the healing of his people. Hans Urs von Balthasar, one of Nietzsche's theological critics, wrote that in Christ we discover that God's "absolute power is identical with absolute self-giving." He comes not to destroy his enemies but to forgive them. He comes not to obliterate broken minds but to bear and heal them.

THE HANDS OF OUR KING ARE, in Tolkien's words, "the hands of a healer."
I read those words in *The Lord of the Rings* during the early, dark days of my illness, as I struggled to come to terms with my precious, hostile mind. I had been waiting for God to act, assuming that would mean an end to my mental illness, an end to the shattered self I had become. I wasn't sure what would be left, but it wouldn't be the self I knew, fragile and bewildered. It was in Aragorn, Tolkien's exiled king, that I glimpsed a God whose power in my life might arrive as a cradling of my broken mind, a healing of my fragmented identity, a bearing of my frailty.

Aragorn, having saved his people from obliteration, has gained the right to enter his city as conqueror and take his throne. But he comes instead, first, as healer. Entering the city by back gates, he slips into the houses where the wounded lie dying, fulfilling an ancient prophecy that "the hands of a king are the hands of a healer." Moving from bed to bed, he draws his people back from the shadowlands of physical or spiritual despair. He heals even his enemy, Faramir, the man who could rival his claim to the throne. When Faramir wakes, he does so with a "light of love" in his eyes and names Aragorn as his king, recognizing him for his humility rather than his capacity to dominate.

That's how I recognized God's arrival in my own story: by a grace and gentle presence that restored and healed me even as it bore the darkness of my broken mind. I barely recognized myself when I emerged, raw and afraid, from

a ghost of my former self, trying to survive by subtraction. I prayed for God to zap everything back to normal and waited, suspended and silent.

But my prayers went unanswered. You cannot heal a broken psyche by destroying it. I gradually discovered that the imagination I had loved in my youth still ached and sang even in the midst of darkness. I found that, almost against my will, God drew me back into the beauty and creativity that had illumined my childhood. Celtic music provoked the ancient and wild joy I had once known. I found that novels led me back to the inward spaces of hope and dreaming I had once inhabited, that fragments of poetry waited for me to form them, that stories hovered on the edge of my consciousness when I sat alone. They came to me like food to the starving.

A nascent understanding took root as I sat in my room during those long, wintry years: my enemy mind was still intimately, irrevocably, bewilderingly . . . me. It was part of myself, an agent capable of both goodness and torment, never to be untangled or separated from my entire being. My prayers for obliteration had been mercifully unanswered, but now I was filled with the realization that I might have to live with something that was both my treasure and my enemy for the rest of my life.

But, as I was just beginning to discover, this is what it means to be human: created for joy yet broken by sin and in need of redemption. It wasn't just my mind but my whole self that was a tangle of glory and disaster, one that God would not discard but cherish, forgive, and heal.

Better than any mythical Aragorn, Jesus actually came and stood human and vulnerable among us. He came by the back door, with the hands of a healer, and he loved us even when we were his enemies. He stood among us, pouring out his life to heal broken minds and diseased bodies, evil hearts and twisted souls, setting free the enemies who would become his redeemed people.

I can almost imagine it. ⤳

the first months of my illness and began the long-term work of coping with my kind of insanity. At first, I let the creative girl I'd been drop away. Imagination was now tinged with terror; it wasn't something I could control and so I rejected it along with the evil images it caused. I stopped journaling, a habit I had cultivated since childhood. I stopped writing stories. I stopped dreaming. I shunned friendship but was also nervous of solitude. I was profoundly diminished,

Daniel Bonnell, *Blue Doves*, mixed media on paper, 2023

Enemy Lovers

Five historical figures respond to real enemies.

Saint John Chrysostom

Etty Hillesum

Martin Luther King Jr.

Thich Nhat Hanh

Christian de Chergé

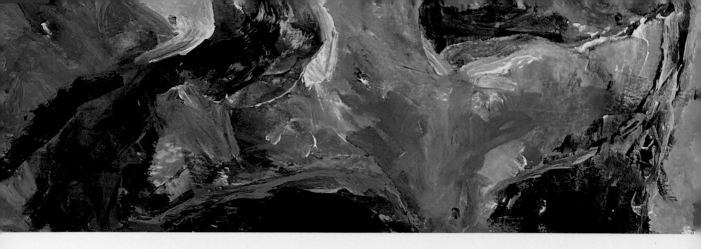

Saint John Chrysostom

As Archbishop of Constantinople in the fourth century, John Chrysostom had his share of enemies. One was Eutropius, an administrator under Emperor Arcadius who denied citizens the right of sanctuary in churches – until AD 399, when he himself landed up on the wrong side of the law and sought refuge at the altar. Rather than turn him in, Chrysostom ensured his safety and even convinced Arcadius to spare Eutropius's life. Below, he explains why.

Wherefore art thou indignant with me? You say it is because he who continually made war upon the church has taken refuge within it. Yet surely we ought to glorify God, for permitting this man to be placed in such a great strait as to experience both the power and the loving-kindness of the church: her power in that he has suffered this great vicissitude in consequence of the attacks which he made upon her; her loving-kindness in that she whom he attacked now casts her shield in front of him and has received him under her wings, and placed him in all security not resenting any of her former injuries, but most lovingly opening her bosom to him. For this is more glorious than any kind of trophy, this is a brilliant victory, this puts both Gentiles and Jews to shame, this displays the bright aspect of the church: in that having received her enemy as a captive, she spares him, and when all have despised him in his desolation, she alone like an affectionate mother has concealed him under her cloak, opposing both the wrath of the king, and the rage of the people. . . .

Has he inflicted great wrongs and insults on you? I will not deny it. Yet this is the season not for judgment but for mercy; not for requiring an account, but for showing loving-kindness; not for investigating claims but for conceding them; not for verdicts and vengeance, but for mercy and favor. Let no one then be irritated or vexed, but let us rather beseech the merciful God to grant him a respite from death, and to rescue him from this impending destruction, so that he may put off his transgression, and let us unite to approach the merciful emperor, beseeching him for the sake of the church, for the sake of the altar, to concede the life of one man. . . . God says, "I will have mercy and not sacrifice," and throughout the scriptures you find him always enquiring after this, and declaring it to be the means of release from sin.

Saint Chrysostom, in *Nicene and Post-Nicene Fathers*, Series 1, Volume 9, Philip Schaff, ed., trans. W. R. W. Stephens (New York: Christian Literature Company, 1889).

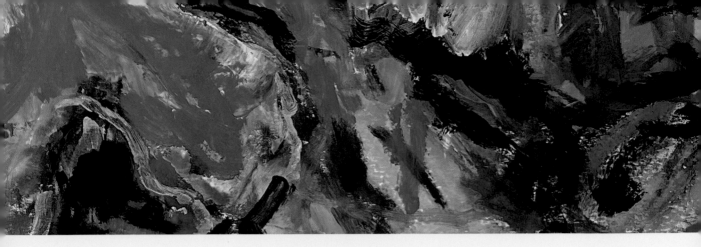

Etty Hillesum

A Dutch Jew, Etty Hillesum is known for her diaries and letters describing the spiritual awakening she underwent in Westerbork, a Nazi transit camp. She was later murdered at Auschwitz.

Scattered through this vast space are a few stoves, which don't even give enough heat for the old ladies crowded around them. How people are expected to live through the winter in these barracks has not yet been made clear. . . .

Leading lights from cultural and political circles in the big cities have also been stranded here on this barren heath five hundred by six hundred meters. With one mighty convulsion all their scenery has collapsed about them, and now they stand around a little hesitantly and awkwardly on this drafty, open stage called Westerbork.

These figures, wrenched from their context, still carry with them the restless atmosphere of a society more complicated than the one we have here. They walk along the thin barbed-wire fence. Their silhouettes move, life-sized and exposed, across the great stretch of sky. You cannot imagine it. Their armor of position, esteem, and property has collapsed, and now they stand in the last shreds of their humanity. They exist in an empty space, bounded by earth and sky, which they must fill with whatever they can find within them – there is nothing else.

One suddenly realizes that it is not enough to be an able politician or a talented artist. In the most extreme distress life demands quite other things. Yes, it is true, our ultimate human values are being put to the test. . . .

This is a very one-sided story. I could have told quite another, filled with hatred and bitterness and rebellion. But rebellion born only when distress begins to affect one personally is no real rebellion and can never bear fruit. And the absence of hatred in no way implies the absence of moral indignation.

I know that those who hate have good reason to do so. But why should we always have to choose the cheapest and easiest way? It has been brought home forcibly to me here how every atom of hatred added to the world makes it an even more inhospitable place. And I also believe – childishly perhaps, but stubbornly – that the earth will become more habitable again only through the love that the Jew Paul described to the citizens of Corinth in the thirteenth chapter of his first letter.

Martin Luther King Jr.

King's well-known commitment to nonviolence as a political weapon grew out of his faith, but there was a good streak of pragmatism in his thinking as well. He knew that those who marched with him in the fight for civil rights would have to live for decades to come with the same people they were now confronting. Only by forgiving their oppressors could they end the "descending spiral of destruction."

Far from being the pious injunction of a utopian dreamer, the command to love one's enemy is an absolute necessity for our survival. Returning hate for hate multiplies hate, adding deeper darkness to a night already devoid of stars. Darkness cannot drive out darkness; only light can do that. Hate cannot drive out hate; only love can do that. Hate multiplies hate, violence multiplies violence, and toughness multiplies toughness in a descending spiral of destruction. Love is the only force capable of transforming an enemy into a friend.

And so to our most bitter opponents we say, "We shall match your capacity to inflict suffering by our capacity to endure suffering. We shall meet your physical force with soul force. Do to us what you will, and we shall continue to love you. We cannot in all good conscience obey your unjust laws, because noncooperation with evil is as much a moral obligation as is cooperation with good. Throw us in jail, and we shall still love you. Send your hooded perpetrators of violence into our community at the midnight hour and beat us and leave us half dead, and we shall still love you. But be ye assured that we will wear you down by our capacity to suffer. One day we shall win freedom, but not only for ourselves. We shall so appeal to your heart and conscience that we shall win *you* in the process, and our victory will be a double victory."

Thich Nhat Hanh

Vietnamese Buddhist Thich Nhat Hanh made headlines in the 1960s alongside Thomas Merton and Martin Luther King Jr. by speaking out against the war that was destroying his country and its people.

During the Vietnam War, there was a lot of suffering and people found themselves in a situation where they had become enemies of each other. In such a situation, you have to find a way to survive and to help others survive. We had to show people the way to act properly, because if you don't have peace within yourself, it is very difficult to work for peace. Our thinking was: the other person is not our enemy; our enemies are misunderstanding, discrimination, violence, hatred, and anger.

If you are filled with anger, you create more suffering for yourself than for the other person. When you are inhabited by the energy of anger, you want to punish, you want to destroy. That is why those who are wise do not want to say anything or do anything while the anger is still in them. So you try to bring peace into yourself first. When you are calm, when you are lucid, you will see that the other person is a victim of confusion, of hate, of violence transmitted by society, by parents, by friends, by the environment. When you are able to see that, your anger is no longer there.

Forgiveness will not be possible until compassion is born in our heart. Even if you want to forgive, you cannot forgive. In order to be compassionate, you have to understand why the other person has done that to you and your people. You have to see that they are victims of their own confusion, their own worldview, their own grieving, their own discrimination, their own lack of understanding and compassion.

Suppose you are angry at your father. Many people are angry at their father, and yet if they don't do anything to change it when they grow up, they will repeat exactly what their father did to them. . . . When you are capable of visualizing your father as a five-year-old boy – fragile, tender, full of wounds – you begin to understand and feel compassion.

An act of compassion always brings about transformation. If not right now, it will happen in the future. The important thing is you don't react with anger. You react with compassion, and sooner or later you see the transformation in the other person.

From an interview with Martin Doblmeier of Journey Films for a documentary broadcast on public television in 2007. Reprinted with permission from *Sojourners, sojo.net.*

Christian de Chergé

Prior of a Cistercian monastery in the Atlas Mountains of Algeria, Christian de Chergé was known for his service to his poor Muslim neighbors. But that was not enough to spare him from being kidnapped and slain, along with six fellow monks, by Islamic terrorists in 1996. De Chergé had anticipated such a fate and written a letter to his future assassin, to be opened after his death.

*I*f it should happen one day – and it could be today – that I become a victim of the terrorism which now seems ready to engulf Algeria, I would like my community, my church, and my family to remember that my life was given to God and to this country. I ask them to accept the fact that the one Master of all life was not a stranger to this brutal departure. I would ask them to pray for me: for how could I be found worthy of such an offering? I ask them to associate this death with so many other equally violent ones which are forgotten through indifference or anonymity. . . .

I should like, when the time comes, to have a moment of spiritual clarity which would allow me to beg forgiveness of God and of my fellow human beings, and at the same time forgive with all my heart the one who would strike me down.

I could not desire such a death. It seems important to state this. I do not see how I could rejoice if the people I love were indiscriminately accused of my murder. . . . Obviously, my death will appear to confirm those who judge me naive or idealistic: "Let him tell us now what he thinks of his ideals!" But these persons should know that finally my most avid curiosity will be set free. This is what I shall be able to do, God willing: immerse my gaze in that of the Father to contemplate with him his children of Islam just as he sees them, all shining with the glory of Christ, the fruit of his Passion, filled with the gift of the Spirit whose secret joy is always to establish communion and restore the likeness, playing with the differences.

For this life lost, totally mine and totally theirs, I thank God, who seems to have willed it. . . . And also you, my last-minute friend, who will not have known what you were doing: Yes, I want this thank you and this goodbye to be a "God bless" for you, too, because in God's face I see yours. May we meet again as happy thieves in paradise, if it please God, the Father of us both. ⤖

"Testament of Christian de Chergé." Translation by Order of Cistercians of the Strict Observance, *ocso.org*.

South Head, a Wild Surmise

Climbing the leaf-hung stairway from the beach,
You step past antique cannon onto a lawn
With benches and a scattering of wrens.
Your eyes are drawn
Across, around the harbour, scanning each
Headland and cove that bends
The haze-bedazzled shoreline, till they reach,

Way off, those glassy towers, the office blocks,
An apparition out of science fiction,
As though the city that you travelled through
Were a prediction,
Not here and now, a temporal paradox
Put up to baffle you.
Then you proceed, up steps cut in the rocks,

Skirting the pilot's cottage, to South Head,
The empty gun emplacements, the lighthouse,
The cliff face dropping sheer into the sea,
With its plosive dowse
Of surge and foam, the wind's unlimited
Onrush of nullity,
Against which you are braced to stand and tread.

If you should lean and reach out into it,
Would that arm too be made of emptiness?
On the way back you come to that bank of lawn
The wrens possess.
This time you watch them as they skitter and flit,
Minutely feeding on
Skerricks around the bench on which you sit.

So used to people are they that they treat
Their passing forms as though they were not there,
The tiny flying insects you can't see
Their only care,
As they flutter and pounce around your stationed feet
So unconcernedly.
Indeed, what is the limit of their petite

And searching eyes? The harbour you survey,
Those distant towers that the sun ignites,
The coloured yachts, may be the merest blur
Beyond their sight's
Brief focus, which dissolves into the day,
Like the stretched arm you were
Imagining the wind might make away.

Photograph: Juergen Wallstabe, *South Head
with Sydney skyline in background.*

STEPHEN EDGAR

Artwork by Carol Aust. Used by permission.

The Witching Hour

We start the day intentionally and prayerfully, but all bets are off after five o'clock p.m., when we close our door to the world and think we've earned a break.

KATHLEEN A. MULHERN

"'TIS NOW THE VERY WITCHING TIME of night," Hamlet declared, even as he was well on his way to the madness of vengeance. This "witching time" empowered him, he said, to "do such bitter business as the day would quake to look on." Shakespeare here drew on medieval ideas about the power of darkness and the blurring of boundaries between the physical and the supernatural that happens at certain times of the night. For ancients, these hours usually fell after

---

Kathleen A. Mulhern is a writer, speaker, and historian. She holds a doctorate in European intellectual history, and teaches Christian formation and church history at Denver Seminary.

Carol Aust, *Shadows*, acrylics on wood panel, 2018.

midnight, well before dawn. Then, it was said, the fairies and imps, goblins and demons would roam freely, doing their witchy works. The natural slept; the supernatural woke and began to prowl.

Some, associating evil with the absolute inversion of good, believed that 3:00 a.m., twelve hours apart from the time at which Jesus died on the cross, was the apex of the witching hours. Some called it "the devil's hour."

I was never taught any of the medieval ways when I was young, but I well remember being told as a young mother that those cranky hours of the early evening when our children, hungry and tired out from the day, ramped up a fussiness that perfectly converged with our own hungers and fatigues, were part of "the witching hour." Dinner, bath, and bedtime were one long battle for patience on everyone's part.

Since those years, I've learned the term comes in handy for a variety of colloquial situations. *The Economist* calls the "witching hour" those after-school hours when juvenile crime actually surges. Healthcare observers suggest that perhaps there is a "witching hour" for the operating rooms in hospitals, during the critical turnover times between surgeries. Stock traders recognize witching hours as well, calling the market instability of certain quarterly periods triple-witching days.

Even in our ultramodern scientific world, there's some sense that greater volatility eddies around us at times, a subliminal precariousness to the order we maintain at other times. We've banished the idea of roaming trolls, but those evening hours, that liminal time between day and night, between work and sleep, between order and chaos remains fraught with a sense of anarchy.

Oddly enough, this "witching hour" construct has recently begun to pop up in the spiritual formation sessions I lead. As we work on such things as developing a rule of life, or consider our personal weaknesses and vices, or explore the rhythms and rituals of spiritual health, I've

repeatedly had people point specifically to the evening hours as a greater challenge to their best intentions. "Such bitter business as the day would quake to look on" seems quite accurate. All bets are off after five o'clock.

Seasons and life stages may differ, but the undergirding sense of evening disruption is common. So, yes, young parents find the hours of five to ten a gauntlet-running experience, rife with

---

Five o'clock is a mini-TGIF, no matter the day, and any sense of spiritual discipline vaporizes into the desperate desire for quiet, a scotch and soda, and some banal Netflix series.

---

cranky children, snippy spouses, dinner preparation and clean-up, baths, bedtime rituals, and exhaustion. But I've also had single adults identify the evening with their frequent inability to keep focused on the presence of Christ, distracted as they are by home chores, the latest basketball series, catching up with email, doomscrolling on their smartphones, watching TikTok videos. I have older students, many of whom are single through loss of a spouse to death or divorce and whose children are long gone from home, who dread the evening hours' long stretches of loneliness and boredom. There are a million good things they *could* do, but they have no desire to do any of them.

There are the businessmen and women who, after a long day of productivity and focus and dealing with people, come home and feel that the workday is done. Now it's "me" time; five o'clock is a mini-TGIF, no matter the day, and any sense of spiritual discipline or Christ-centeredness vaporizes into the desperate desire for quiet, a scotch and soda, and some banal Netflix series. Happy hour is the off-switch of work and the on-switch of leisure. "I've done well today. I've worked hard. I've given my max . . . and now I'm tapped. I'm done. I'm out."

I'm not denying the need for genuine rest or "recharging your batteries" or "letting your hair down." But the challenge of living with the Spirit is real in both the workplace (the morning and

---

Part of the diagnosis lies in the fact that we think of spiritual discipline as work, a sort of spiritual productivity, not as the avenue of spiritual rest.

---

afternoon business of your life) and the home (the space after the door closes on the world). We needn't believe that demons roam our kitchens and living rooms to recognize that many of us struggle to maintain our spiritual disciplines by the end of the day.

Part of the diagnosis must lie in the fact that we think of spiritual discipline as work, a sort of spiritual productivity, not as the avenue of spiritual rest. Spiritual disciplines are used as self-management techniques, achievement markers, or DIY transformation tools rather than as openings for the Spirit. Meanwhile, "leisure" has morphed from a gift of the Spirit for our renewal into merely entertainment and pleasure. The spiritual life is hard work, right? We all need "time off." The home space, then, creates a freedom and privacy that allows us to embrace our carnal selves without anyone else seeing.

After all, who can sustain twenty-four-hour godliness?

Even that has problems. We're real people with real limitations, some of which include the chasm between our genuine spiritual desire and our best efforts. And none of us who live the "mixed life," as medieval writers called a life that wasn't cloistered, can bridge that gap. That leaves us peering into the crevices of our crisscrossed lives and pondering the murky shadows. Many of those shadows sharpen and darken once the sun begins to set.

So those of us who guide others in pursuing spiritual formation should consider the "witching hours" a particular challenge and opportunity. We often encourage intentional mornings, advising people to set the trajectory of their day with morning prayers and quiet times. And it's common to promote one-line "arrow prayers" that redirect our attention to God in situations throughout the workday. But seizing these diminishing hours of the day might be a new focus, even more countercultural.

There's no need to turn "the witching hour" into a nightly occasion of self-flagellation and shame. Rather, it's an opportunity to explore different ways of formation, recognizing that what "works" from nine to five might not toward the end of the day. Any spiritual formation practice is, essentially, a way of interrupting the daily rhythms that keep us too busy to remember God. So we may need to look for ways to interrupt evening distractions as well. These interruptions can be smaller than we think. We're not trying to transform our evenings into five-hour prayer sessions; we're just trying to remain mindful of God's presence.

Many have found some of the monastic rhythms readily adaptable to their evening hours. Vespers (evening prayer around sunset) and compline (just before bed) can bookend the hours with moments of awareness that defuse the disorder we may feel. Others find that the Ignatian

spiritual practice of examen, a brief examination of conscience, offers renewal no matter what has happened during the evening hours.

I encourage people to start small. Do one little thing, and do it until it's a regular little thing: light a candle at twilight and give thanks to God for the day; kneel beside your bed in silence before God for five minutes before you get in; say the Lord's Prayer each night – with your spouse or children; sing the doxology before dinner; choose one evening a week to forgo regular habits and dedicate an hour to spiritual reading. Do that little thing that you're most capable of doing. No heroics necessary. Parents of young children will quickly realize that the little rituals are the most meaningful ones – that might last a lifetime.

When my children were young, I found that the nature of their play changed toward evening. From making blanket forts or Hot Wheel racing lanes in the living room, they would begin to bring their play into the kitchen. Stuffed animals and Legos moved under the kitchen table and then into the center of the kitchen floor. I realized at some point that they were simply moving closer to me. As I prepared dinner and twilight fell and they anticipated their dad getting home, they swirled around me, closer and closer until they were right underfoot. They simply knew the day was nearly done and they needed me more. I was going to feed them and tuck them in.

In the same way, we, like little children, need to recognize these evening hours as opportunities to creep closer to Christ, knowing our weaknesses and our hungers, and trusting him to care for us.

Carol Aust, *Single Candle*, acrylic on panel, 2022.

Fatimetu Bushraya and Endoruha Farkun, members of the Saharawi Mine Action Team.

Meet the Algerian women replacing landmines with trees.

Demining the Sahara

**Photo essay by
Maria Novella De Luca**

With text by Alice Pistolesi
and Monica Pelliccia

Begun in 2019, the Saharawi Mine Action Team (SMAWT) is an association of women engaged in demining activities along the Moroccan-built sand wall, or berm, that runs about 1,600 miles from Mauritania through Western Sahara to Morocco, and along Morocco's border with Algeria. The territory remains the longest continuously mined area in the world, estimated to hold between seven and ten million landmines.

The Saharawi people, caught up in decades of territorial struggle over Western Sahara, still wait to return to their lands, occupied by Morocco since 1974.

Acacia trees taking root in Saharawi Liberated Territories (as seen through a camera lens).

Among them, women like Teslem Rgaibi, Endoruha Farkun, and Fatimetu Bushraya work tirelessly for mine reduction and to help the families of those who have been killed or injured: there have been more than 2,500 landmine casualties over the last fifty years. Despite their limited resources, these women have already helped train 3,850 people on the dangers of landmines.

In addition, they aim to regreen the refugee camps scattered along the border by replacing some of the extracted mines with trees that provide wood, shade, and forage for grazing animals, as well as antiseptic and other medicines.

In November 2020, with the resumption of the conflict between the Polisario Front and Morocco, the deminers' activity became even more complicated and dangerous. However, this has not stopped the women of the SMAWT.

Maria Novella De Luca is a freelance photo-journalist who collaborates with NGOs for the creation of social and travel documentary photos and videos.

Alice Pistolesi is an Italian journalist whose work focuses on the conditions of oppressed populations and on environmentalist and feminist protest movements.

Monica Pelliccia is an Italian freelance multimedia journalist who covers environmental and social issues such as biodiversity conservation, women's issues, climate change, indigenous peoples' rights, food security, and agroecology.

Fatimetu Bushraya and Teslem Rgaibi prepare for a demining operation.

Teslem Rgaibi, twenty-four, lives with her mother, father, and sister. She proudly carries on her demining job despite the resumption of the conflict.

"Our task is to spread awareness to an increasing number of people, especially among the displaced," she explains. She gives particular value to their education campaign: a higher awareness of the risk posed by mines means possibly saving lives.

"Once, I met with a woman, alone in her house. When we started talking about the dangers she started crying, remembering her dead brother. That's why I would like to spread information about mines as much as I can. Because at the end this is what really matters: to help people avoid war hazards and ultimately save their lives."

Before the conflict heated up again, she and other women were growing seedlings of acacia, the local thorn trees, for replanting throughout the demined area, a project she hopes to revive soon.

Endoruha Farkun conducts a search for landmines.

Endoruha Farkun, thirty-two, has been part of the group since its foundation. She was already planting trees in the refugee camp.

"When we are demining," she says, "we wake up very early to reach the minefield at the crack of dawn and start searching for the bombs together with the specialized group." Farkun lives with her father, grandmother, and three sisters. "My family is very proud of what I do and has always supported me. It gives me great satisfaction to find bombs, remove them, and destroy them. I feel that I am doing something important, that I have contributed to erasing a danger that could have killed one or more people. At first I was very scared, but when I start working, I concentrate and only think of what I have to do."

Fatimetu Bushraya with her son

Fatimetu Bushraya, thirty-five, was pregnant when she started working as a deminer in 2019. "I continued to demine even when I was expecting my first child; I knew it could be dangerous, but I felt I had to do it for future generations."

Along with the entire team, Bushraya is waiting for the conflict to subside so they can resume the demining activity. "I know that this is dangerous and hard work. Because we are in a male-dominated society, I had to overcome the strict opposition of my father and brothers to become a deminer. The difficulties that I feel the most are certainly the time spent far from our families, the tough weather conditions, and of course being in dangerous places every day, full of mines, where a wrong step can cost your life." ⤳

Just Doing What Christians Do

Forgiving beheaders, praying for enemies – it's a daily reality for Coptic Christians.

ARCHBISHOP ANGAELOS

The Coptic Orthodox Archbishop of London speaks with Plough's *Alan Koppschall about the Copts' outsized witness as a persecuted religious minority in Egypt.*

Alan Koppschall: Christ calls his followers to love their enemies and those who persecute them. The Coptic Church has had to reckon with that radical enemy love in a way that almost no other church in the present age

has. If we go back to the aftermath of the Arab Spring in Egypt and the political turmoil that followed, how did this affect your church and what was the response of the Coptic Christians?

Archbishop Angaelos: At the time of the uprising in Egypt, as was the case across the Middle East, there was a lot of unrest and uncertainty. Some people had high hopes of achieving political reform, others were anxious and hesitant. Others

Mosaic mural at the entrance to Saint Virgin Mary's Coptic Orthodox Church in Cairo, Egypt.

were trying to push a personal agenda. And so for Christians it was important to continue to be Christians throughout, and that is to be constructive members of society: to be prayerful and hopeful but also strong and faithful.

At one stage, when the political situation was very tense, Islamists tried to break society apart by attacking Christians – expecting Christians would attack them in return and thereby instigate a civil war. And so, in August 2013, there were attacks on a hundred churches and places of Christian ministry across Egypt within a forty-eight-hour window. It was obviously orchestrated. And the remarkable thing was that in an incredibly inflamed political environment – it was an absolute tinderbox and anything could have ignited it – there was not one single retaliation, violent or otherwise, against any of these attacks.

No communication went out from the patriarchate or the diocese saying, "Don't retaliate." It was just Christians in Egypt doing what the Christians in Egypt do. And by not retaliating, they took the wind out of that initiative. By the admission of many, including political analysts and non-Christians at every level, that's what protected the community.

The Coptic Church was brought onto the world stage more recently through the terrible act of violence carried out by ISIS against twenty-one migrant workers on a Libyan beach in February 2015. How did this incident help to demonstrate the importance of loving one's enemies?

That was a pivotal point, I think, that impacted many people around the world, religious and nonreligious. It was an act of such inhumanity that it crossed a line that many were not ready to cross. The impact the executions made had two sources. The first was the men themselves, the twenty Coptic Christians and their Ghanaian friend. Their resilience, their strength, their utterance of the name of Christ to the very end was a real display of grace.

Just as in the Book of Daniel the three young men in the fiery furnace had a fourth with them, I am sure there was a twenty-second man on that beach. Christ must have been in their midst because their peace was visible on their faces.

The second reason the execution made such an impact was the reaction of the victims' families.

Just as in the Book of Daniel the three young men in the fiery furnace had a fourth with them, I am sure there was a twenty-second man on that beach.

The German novelist Martin Mosebach was so moved by the story that he traveled to Egypt to write his book *The 21: A Journey into the Land of Coptic Martyrs* (Plough, 2019). He went to live with the families, expecting to see people broken by an act that had taken away their men, but he found them celebrating their witness and forgiving the perpetrators. I think that was an eye opener.

When word of the executions first reached Britain, I had over thirty interviews in the twenty-four hours following the announcement. And all the interviewers asked me, "How can you possibly forgive?" Because in my first interview I had spoken about forgiving the perpetrators. It was such a countercultural, counterintuitive sentiment. And I think it was another display of grace. It is the grace of God in us that allows us to love as he loves and to forgive as he forgives.

Archbishop Angaelos serves as the Coptic Orthodox Archbishop of London and Papal Legate to the United Kingdom.

Forgiveness is tied into loving God – which includes loving ourselves as the image and likeness of God. Because it is in seeing that image and likeness within us and within everybody else, including our enemies, that we are then led to love and to forgive everybody. Not forgiving the action itself but the person committing the action; never justifying or accepting the hostility itself but recognizing human brokenness and realizing that we're all broken and all need God's forgiveness. In recognizing that, we can begin to love the image and likeness of God in the perpetrators, forgive them, and pray for them that their broken humanity could one day be restored.

Jesus' commandment to love our enemies doesn't just apply in the most extreme cases. It needs to be something that we live in our everyday lives. As a member of a church that has suffered so much persecution, how do you show love to your enemies on a daily basis?

We tend to romanticize the big things – like the twenty-one martyrs, or the sacrifice of missionaries in far corners of the world. But in fact, day-to-day life, in Britain or anywhere else, means having to love those who persecute us or even just make our lives slightly more uncomfortable on a daily basis. We have to continue to live our faith, the "faith that carries us," because forgiveness doesn't come out of a vacuum: forgiveness is based on love, and love is based on understanding the nature of God, who is in and of himself love. In scripture we're told he loves us first. And when we have that realization, we're able to see how much he loves us – and how much he has forgiven us. And how many times, as with the adulterous woman or the paralytic or others he met, he will say to us, "Your sins are forgiven. Go and sin no more." And yet we do sin again, and he will meet us again with the same grace and the same love. So I think it's very important for us to continue to live the message of our Lord Jesus Christ and continue to walk in his footsteps.

What about the imprecatory psalms? How should we reconcile love of enemies with the chanting of these psalms that seem to invoke judgment, calamity, and curses upon one's enemies?

The beautiful thing about our scriptures is that they're not sanitized. They don't tell us we're never going to have a problem. When the psalmist is in the depths of anxiety he says: "How long, O Lord, will you forget me?" When he is in the depths of need, he says: "I will lift up my eyes to the hills." When he is in the depths of the darkness of the journey of life, he speaks of journeying through the valley of death – with the protection of the staff and the rod of the shepherd. All of these things are human emotions God encourages us to express in human terms.

From a mosaic mural at the entrance to Saint Virgin Mary's Coptic Orthodox Church in Cairo, Egypt.

So, no, we don't use the psalms to curse, and we don't use the psalms to vent. We are using the psalms to place our pain before God, because the psalms are communication with God to put our petitions before the Lord who will answer us. People sometimes weaponize scripture using verses taken out of context to justify anger and hostility. But the culmination of scripture in both the Old and New Testaments is the victory of God's love, the victory of good over evil and of life over death.

What should the church do in response to the war in Ukraine?

Pray. The church must offer up prayers for those who are adversely affected, for those in power, for people who are on the frontline, for all the people who suffer. Where the church can speak a good word to de-escalate or bring reconciliation, we should do that. Much of what we do will not have an immediate effect, because these wars are based on geopolitics and national interests, which people are less than willing to let go of. But we must certainly never add fuel to the fire, and we must never be a cause of greater enmity. The church has to be a presence of hope and peace.

Jesus himself doesn't tell us not to have enemies. He himself had many and still has many enemies. How do we stick uncompromisingly to the truth of the gospel while still loving our enemies?

I've struggled with this concept of "the enemy" for many years and have come to the understanding that while I myself do not have enemies, there are people in the world who consider themselves my enemy. But even so, I must still love them.

In terms of what we do, we need to be honest with ourselves. One of the requirements for a successful dialogue is to dialogue about the right thing in the right way at the right time. And so there are things we are not going to agree on, even among Christians. There are some things I, as a Coptic Orthodox Christian, cannot compromise on. Ego, status, power – all of those things we can and should compromise on. When it comes to doctrine, there are things we cannot compromise

---

We tend to romanticize the big things – like the twenty-one martyrs, or the sacrifice of missionaries in far corners of the world. But day-to-day life means having to love those who persecute us or even just make our lives slightly more uncomfortable on a daily basis.

---

on, but these also do not stop us from living side by side. And they do not stop us from witnessing together and living the love and grace of our Lord together – being the "light of the world."

Praying for your enemies is also an important part of the gospel, isn't it?

Absolutely. We need to pray for everything and everyone, which includes praying, as our Lord did, for those who consider themselves our enemies. Even when he was on the cross, he prayed for his executioners, saying: "Forgive them, Father, for they know not what they do." When speaking of those who are perpetrators of atrocities, there's an element of such people "not knowing what they do" because they are hitting out at what they consider to be a dehumanized entity, whereas in reality, they're attacking a full human being, someone who holds the image and likeness of God. ⤳

MARY TOWNSEND

Hating Sinners

*Love the sinner and hate the sin? The trouble is,
that's not how hatred works.*

IN *THE GENEALOGY OF MORALITY*, Nietzsche describes the intensity of glee that second-century author Tertullian experienced when he imagined what might go on in hell. "What there excites my admiration? What my derision?" Tertullian writes. "Which sight gives me joy? Which rouses me to exultation?" Well, it turns out that for him, it's the sight of actors, poets, playwrights, even a poor charioteer, and of course some philosophers "tossing in the fiery billows," glowing in "the dissolving flame" – that is to say, a collection of his fellow humans literally roasting in hell.

Nietzsche finds Tertullian's exultation to be a perfect example for one of his more trenchant critiques of Christianity, based on Nietzsche's notion of the kind of slow-burning ire he dubs "ressentiment." The trouble with ressentiment, Nietzsche thinks, is that it is a species of anger that comes from a negation, saying no to what is outside, other, and different from one's self. Ressentiment wants scapegoats to pin all our shortcomings on, to have something to destroy to try to make ourselves feel a little better, like the angry neighbors in Shirley Jackson's *We Have Always Lived in the Castle* (1962), or for that matter, the Nazis justifying mass murder of the Jews.

If Nietzsche were correct that this is simply the sum and substance of the Christian view of enmity and sin, of the wicked and of sinners, he would certainly have a point. If ressentiment is not just an occasional failing of individuals who didn't quite get the message, but really at the root of what we Christians say when we reach for truisms like Augustine's "love the sinner, hate the sin," something would be amiss in the very nature of the love expressed in the Gospels.

Fortunately, Nietzsche is *not* correct. The overwhelming divine love that, as Dante puts it, moves the very stars can be experienced and expressed even by mere mortals. But there is a problem here that remains, both for the human and the Christian, about what to do in the face of things we honestly want to name as, well, bad – and not just kind of bad, but really and truly wicked. We can safely say that Tertullian's enjoyment of poets glowing in the flames, especially given that he himself eventually renounced Christianity proper for the prophecies of Montanus, is simply not a good example. But is renouncing evil enough, or

is there a way in which anger or even hatred could be appropriate?

Is there a way to hate without falling into the trap that Nietzsche identifies, where ressentiment becomes not just the source of our indignation but the substance of what we claim to love as well?

In PSALM 58, the psalmist writes of the wicked, saying wistfully:

Let them vanish like water that runs away;
Like grass let them be trodden down and wither.
Let them be like the snail that dissolves into slime.

There's something deeply appealing in this description of the snail – the satisfaction of imagining a wicked person reduced to a smaller and smaller trail of glistening snail snot. It's touching somehow, or at least bathetic, even if stronger images precede and follow it; earlier on in the psalm, the human voice prays for God to break the very teeth of the wicked; later, the psalmist has the righteous "bathe their feet in the blood" of the same.

But perhaps because the psalmist's descriptions are more baroque, or at least more human-scaled than Tertullian's fire, with things like grass, teeth, feet, water, and snails – and crucially, set

---

Mary Townsend serves as assistant professor of philosophy at St. John's University and is the author of The Woman Question in Plato's Republic *(Lexington Books, 2017).*

on the earth we know rather than the hell we imagine – they at least rescale the problem into something easier to investigate. Unlike consigning enemies to cosmic fire in an unknowable afterlife, they allow us to begin to understand the right response to evil by thinking about the psychologically recognizable moments of individuals.

One human phenomenon that the psalmist returns to again and again in his prayers is the strange experience of one human taking another for an enemy.

> Deliver me from my enemies, O my God
> Protect me from those who rise up against me.
> Deliver me from those who work evil;
> From the bloodthirsty save me.
> For even now, they lie in wait for my life.
> (Psalm 59)

Is not the devil the true enemy, and our fellow human, as the saying goes, our neighbor? And yet, who has not been at least tempted by something like the following absurd progression? Picture a person on the floor above you making too much noise – so annoying! – and unneighborly, too, it might seem. But now consider the shift where you begin to regard this neighbor not as a cause of anger, but the *focus* of anger, not just a person who occasionally wears heavy boots indoors, but someone who works evil. To me, what makes someone, a hitherto ordinary person, into an enemy is the difference between a "no big deal" and what my children and students might call "drama." An enemy is no longer simply a person, but a Public Nuisance. The small anger you experience becomes steady and starts to take on that inveterate quality of hatred.

Of course, real enemies, even within peaceful times, do exist; and although it may sound sophistical to say so, you could hardly attempt to love your enemies if they were not around for you to do so. Perhaps the person with the boots has decided for some reason to hate your guts; or one thing you said on day one pissed off your freshman college roommate forever.

These examples are purposefully trivial in order to highlight that no one involved is necessarily *wicked*. But once you have made an enemy, his or her presence even at a distance is undeniable, and unforgettable. When your enemies are elsewhere, you imagine that they are really lying in wait for you, as the psalmist describes, on the other side of the telephone, the internet, the island. That they would be bloodthirsty only in a metaphorical way is hardly a full consolation.

ASIDE FROM NEIGHBORS and roommates, consider also the notion of the professional enemy. There is no better lighthearted poem about this species of enmity than Clive James's poem "The Book of My Enemy Has Been Remaindered," where the profession is that of the professional author, and his enemy, the literary sort.

> The book of my enemy has been remaindered
> And I am pleased.
> In vast quantities it has been remaindered
> Like a van-load of counterfeit that has been seized
> And sits in piles in a police warehouse,
> My enemy's much-prized effort sits in piles
> In the kind of bookshop where remaindering occurs.
> Great, square stacks of rejected books.

If you are not an author yourself, this kind of bookish rivalry might seem somewhat odd. Yet as Plato's Diotima notes, poets are even more attached to their poems than parents to their children. And the funny thing is, once you are willing to take up the author's conceit, it becomes somehow not unpleasant to imagine the book, specifically of someone you have run afoul of, to have been rejected to the extent that it no longer makes sense to even *try* to sell a new copy at full price to anyone, at all. In fact, there would be a certain dishonesty to *not* admitting the sort of pleasure that James's poem records. And certainly, it's obvious enough that this sort of professional rivalry extends to many a profession; as Aristotle invokes the Greek proverb, potters never agree. But who is this book-enemy of the poem, and where did he come from? And most importantly, what did he *do* to deserve the title of enemy?

In James's poem, the enemy has no whence or whither; he simply arrives full-fledged, which is part of the satisfying whimsy involved. You're asked to imagine an enemy with no strings attached. In fact, this imaginative act reveals that a certain amount of the enjoyment of the professional enemy comes from an aestheticization of the experience. It's a dream-image of some light-hearted evildoer, whose crime is unimportant and slightly unreal, like having a villain with an overdone mustache and a silly hat.

Indeed, I have even heard it argued among authors of my acquaintance that it is pleasant to do a certain amount of conscious cultivation of this sort, taking an ordinary human with whom you have a vague rivalry, and enjoying the sensation of imagining this person into something of more importance, someone to scheme about, to rejoice or moan at any failure or triumph. Partly, this is a way of keeping yourself on your toes, particularly if other people happen to have picked you to cultivate as their own cheerful enemy-project. It also gives you a sense of importance, as someone distinguished enough to have an enemy, as you might own a particularly expensive watch. (Of course, this elevates the importance of the enemy as well.)

But amidst all this comedy, it should be obvious that it is terrible, actually, to have a real enemy, and probably worse than having a testy neighbor. It is no fun to get a nasty email, or even to be cut from a party, not to mention if someone tries to get you fired, or spreads malicious gossip.

This shift from the comically desirable to the truthfully unpleasant is even clearer when real, physical violence comes into play. No one forgets

---

Hatred reifies things as it goes, creates demons where there are none, animates evil from situations where there were only mistakes or even simply ordinary ambiguities.

---

the real school bully, and not because it was fun to be pinched when the teacher wasn't looking, or glamorous of the bully to do the pinching. Once you're faced with wounds, death, and corpses – as, for example, soldiers are – the cuteness of violence

immediately dissipates, as if there has been a sudden departure of a little haze. In Iris Murdoch's 1961 novel *A Severed Head*, after one character punches an incestuous psychoanalyst in the face, as hard as he can, Murdoch as narrator remarks that "violence, except on the screen, is always pathetic, ludicrous, and beastly," and this is true, even though the incestuous psychoanalyst was not exactly without fault. It's just that, the thing is, there's nothing actually glamorous about being punched in the face. My bet is that this goes for the wish of the psalmist to bathe his feet in the blood of his enemies as well: sounds good in a poem, but in practice unlovely, and also kind of gross.

So why then does that temptation to invest in something as really dangerous as an enemy remain? Consider what *making* an enemy out of someone concretely does to the shape of your soul. In a sense, to pin the tail on the donkey of a rival in this way animates something that was not, strictly speaking, alive before. Hence the saying to "have an animus" for someone, so much does hatred seem to be creative in its energies. This creative energy even extends to actual inanimate

objects – when something as banal as a toaster or the kitchen sink doesn't act as you like it, you treat it as though that toaster had a self, a self you could blame for your burnt toast.

In this way, hatred makes something out of nothing – the stranger irony being that hatred itself, as Aristotle notes, is the very wish that something would vanish from or be destroyed out of existence, forever. In fact, the phenomenon is deeply self-contradictory: hatred is aggrieved at the very existence of what it hates; but to cultivate enmity for the sake of having an enemy is to create the very thing you claim to wish to destroy.

And so the feeling goes around and around, without human end. To contradict Graham Greene, hatred is not a failure of the imagination, it is the imagination's creative act, and it fills the mind so strongly that no rival image or imagining will put an end to it. We are continually creating golems of whom we must live in fear.

This is why it's very important for Christians not to pin too much on Augustine's wildly popular maxim that one way out of the difficulties of enmity is simply to hate the sin, yet not the sinner, "with due love for the persons, and hatred of the sins." The trouble is, that's not how hatred works. Hatred reifies things as it goes, creates demons where there are none, animates evil from situations where there were only mistakes or even simply ordinary ambiguities. Hatred *makes* fake persons; it therefore also makes the real person harder to see. It cements a picture of human life that renders the fundamental ambiguities of ethical life nearly invisible. Like the fancy villain with his mustache and cloak, it aestheticizes the violence with which an entire culture is assigned to the grave by the grave.

Wicked deeds are real, and people can on occasion commit enough of them to be wicked themselves. But the logic of hatred appeals to our wish to avoid the burden of careful judgment; indeed, it turns imprudent human judgment into

an upside-down simulacrum of what God alone can see, let alone decide.

BUT WHAT HAPPENS when Christians have been persuaded that it is best to avoid enmity toward persons and sins, but still want to do more than dissent from the large-scale evils of the world? In allowing in your heart any hatred of abstract principles, false metaphysics, or even your least favorite Christian denomination, I still think there's a risk of conjuring enemies where there were none. To renounce the devil and all his works will involve more than vivifying new cosmic devils, lest we become devils ourselves.

This risk was remarkably well dramatized in an off-Broadway play I recently saw, though this meant that the story ended up being almost more terrifying than I could handle. Samuel D. Hunter's *A Bright New Boise* (original production 2010, revival 2023) is about a man who left his church and started a new job at Hobby Lobby, where as it happens, his teenage biological son also works, whom he has not known but intends now to befriend. His former church was built around the imminence of Armageddon, and despite his departure, he still agrees that something about the modern world will be solved by its destruction. He prays for this, repeatedly. He is upset that it does not happen right away.

For most of the play, it is not quite clear what the man thinks about his old church. Sometimes he lies a little bit about it, and sometimes he does not. The actor did an extraordinary job of portraying someone whose mind is always a little elsewhere; and who, it emerges, is captivated by a cosmic metaphysic that he does much to conceal. But in the end, he can't help but fully express his true contempt for the world, for Idaho, and for the

---

> There's a way in which humanity has become a new sort of vessel once God introduces himself in human form to the world, but plenty of moments of natural man remain. We pray the psalmists' prayers because they are often our prayers too.

---

people who inhabit it. At one point he yells at a Lutheran, right in her face: she's going to hell, he says. (It is because she is too nice.)

When the man finally openly prayed for Armageddon, for the light of the earth to be put out forever, so that a few elect souls would turn into souls of eternal light, it was as though he wanted in some sense to become demonic and almost achieved it.

This moment is painfully far from the way I was raised, though it did remind me a little of a Baptist tent revival I went to with a friend in middle school. The preacher drew little souls falling into hell that we couldn't see while he talked, until other lights being dimmed, he finally shone a black light upon them. Nothing says the aestheticization of retribution better than black light manifesting

the neon blue of the silvery soul; it was a moment indeed of general relish. In *A Bright New Boise*, however, no one relishes destruction quite like the main character, except perhaps his son, the only one who's been willing to listen to his theories. The play ends when the man refuses to see his son after the son attempts suicide; he prefers to continue to pray for universal fire, by himself.

Watching the audience, which after a point I was fairly scared of doing, I wasn't sure what they were thinking. We were all rapt by the action on stage; but something in our common experience left me unsettled. How many times have I heard people on the East Coast wish Idaho didn't exist? Or Alabama, or you name it, or Louisiana, where I'm from? The audience has to reckon with the fact that they in no small part identify with the almost-demon: they too hate flyover country, they too hate the company that the characters all work for, and they too wish the meaningless (as they think) lives of these people into oblivion. Sitting there in New York, by some views the pinnacle of civilization, I wondered if the audience got the joke.

What kept me up at night when it was over was the hollow look in the man's eyes in the moments he was still pretending not to have contempt for what he saw in front of him. Love would not look like that, even or especially love that was honest. But then, what would it look like instead?

What the play left out of the story is that there is an option left between the beauty of a country where, as the store manager puts it, one can make a hundred percent profit selling quilting materials and silk flowers to bozos, and the desire to put an end to this misery as quickly as possible. This absent alternative has something to do with God's love, which is neither hateful nor "nice," and which doesn't wish us to keep our cosmic thoughts hidden until they explode.

But attempting to channel our hatred into even the most abstract principle – say, for example,

secularism or, for that matter, bad urban planning – ends up in the same place as the attempt to hate "the sin." It volatizes the desire to point the blaming finger into a madness that spares nothing from being wrapped into our thirst for destruction. Needless to say, "love" that is based on some ostensible opposition to the hated principle is no true love at all.

I F GOD'S INDESCRIBABLE LOVE does not permit us to consign our fellows to the flames, or wish to destroy the earth, where does our smaller but lingering, all-too-human enjoyment of snail slime leave us?

If we are to avoid the smoldering danger of Nietzsche's ressentiment, one of the most immediate practical things we can do is *not* to ignore these moments as they happen, or to pretend they come from more noble feelings, let alone Christian ones. As Kierkegaard puts it in *Philosophical Fragments*, there's a way in which humanity has become a new sort of vessel once God introduces himself in human form to the world; but on the other hand, plenty of moments of natural man remain. We pray the psalmists' prayers because they are often our prayers too.

On the other hand, the admission of this truth is the beginning of greater love, not its natural limit. In recognizing the comedy in our lust for snail slime, anger can spark off and dissipate lightly, without becoming subterranean or animating small things into zombie-hates. In the Gospel of John, when the authorities come to arrest Jesus, Peter gets mad. He takes a sword and cuts off one of the men's ears, his burst of anger taking an absurd turn. An ear here is a relatively small act of human revenge, an image of pure pettiness, an ear in exchange for the betrayal of the Savior of the world. But what does Jesus do? He puts the ear right back on, an impossibly small but loving miracle, a comedic act of beyond-the-human human love. ⟿

The author would like to thank Dan Walden, Veery Huleatt, and Paul Kirkland for their helpful conversations.

How God Sees Us

We must learn to see the divine worth in everyone regardless of how they treat us.

CHRISTOPH FRIEDRICH BLUMHARDT

OUR WORK MUST FOLLOW two laws. We may not bear grudges against anyone, for the kingdom of God is God's love for all people. And we must not annoy, scorn, or despise any of the poor as of less value than ourselves. You are yourself a miserable wretch if you treat them as though they were of no value. We must always have God's values before our eyes. God's treasure lies within each person, not with the great and powerful of this earth. I even have to say to a king, an emperor, or a general: "As head of state or as a great scholar you have no value before God, only as a poor human being you are of value to him. Your value is not a hair more than that of the humble and poor, of the lowest errand boy."

The divine worth in any despised person must be recognized, and we must protect and cherish it. Whenever we get together with people, we need to consider their value for the kingdom of God. If anyone sins against us or insults, punches, or swears at us, we should not think about the cursing, but be mindful. We could say: "He is foolish insulting me like that." We can even tell him directly: "Hey, it's stupid to curse like that!" But we should not despise him for insulting us because in God's name we see him as precious for the kingdom of heaven.

When history, which confuses us and creates enemies, comes to an end and deception has been driven out of the world, we might see this treasure shining clearly. In the meantime, I must see it in my enemy as a mustard seed and forgive again and again. If someone should insult me a hundred times I must still see in him value for God.

This is what people have not yet learned, and I believe that this is why the kingdom of God has not yet come. People bite and scratch, warring against each other, despising and scorning one another. Even the finest people are ready, for the sake of their beliefs and convictions, to judge and condemn others – they have thoroughly learned that! But to discern what is of God in the enemy, to grasp God's worth in those who insult us, in foreigners, in those far from us who think differently, in the poor just as much as in the noble – this they have not learned.

Only the attitude that Jesus represents can achieve something. Let us learn to be people who can forgive, even seven times a day. We must firmly believe that each person, just as they are, is destined for the kingdom of God, so let us stop judging and condemning them. ➤

Excerpted from a sermon given October 29, 1899, published in Christoph Friedrich Blumhardt, *Ihr Menschen seid Gottes!* (Zurich: Rotapfel Verlag, 1928), translated by Jörg Barth and Renate Barth.

Christoph Friedrich Blumhardt (1842–1919) was a German pastor who influenced theologians such as Dietrich Bonhoeffer, Eberhard Arnold, and Karl Barth. Plough *publishes several books of his writings including* Action in Waiting, Everyone Belongs to God, Evening Prayers, *and* Make Way for the Spirit.

Eric Drooker, *Flood*, scratchboard, watercolor, and colored pencil, 2002

Macedonia Morning

*A decade before the protest movements of
the sixties, radical visionaries were laying a
foundation in the hills of Georgia.*

DANA WISER

"Staughton Lynd, though he would never admit it, is one of the visible saints of the modern American left. . . . Nonviolence was the kernel of almost everything good in the New Left. No one, save King himself, seemed to live and breathe it better than Staughton Lynd." —Paul Buhle, The Nation, 1997

STAUGHTON LYND was at the pinnacle of his fame when he sat quietly in his Chicago living room, considering his future. The 1960s were flaming out in violence. His friends were calling police "pigs," militarizing protests, and employing hatred in the class struggle. The movements he led were taking directions he disagreed with. "I decided that day to give up my place on the speaker's platform and remain true to my beliefs," he told me in 2015. "I opted for obscurity."

Lynd died November 17, 2022. Obituaries noted that he had taught history at Yale, directed civil rights projects, and shaken up international politics. What beliefs would eclipse such accomplishments?

The answer lies in a secluded Appalachian valley. What the *New York Times* obituary passes off as three years in a "Quaker commune in northern Georgia" was key to Lynd's formation. Along Shoal Creek in Habersham County, a few young pacifists gathered after World War II and idealistically set out to build a new society. "The values to which we committed ourselves at Macedonia are the values we sought to live by thereafter," wrote Staughton with his wife, Alice, in their 2009 memoir *Stepping Stones*.

MACEDONIA COOPERATIVE COMMUNITY began as the brainchild of Morris Mitchell, a professor at Columbia University's New College who convened a series of Quaker work camps to benefit poor mountain folk. One project was to start a dairy herd. My father, Art Wiser, traveled from Ithaca, New York, during the summer of

---

Dana Wiser is a member of the Bruderhof. He lives with his wife in Pennsylvania.

Staughton Lynd cleans up after the cows, ca. 1956.

bother him anymore, and how that night an FBI agent and a sheriff's posse hauled him out of bed and patted him down for weapons. How Dorothy Boddie, later Mommsen, a refined Southern girl, demanded to know if there were any more "gentlemen" out there after yet another lawman had stepped over her sleeping on the porch to arrest the pacifist inside.

More idealists found their way to Macedonia. They built cabins and shared the scanty living provided by the dairy and the worn-out farmland. After several business ventures failed, two teachers visiting from Atlanta suggested they make wooden toys, and in 1947 the Macedonia community started making unit blocks in a living room. Soon the workshop expanded into a chicken barn, where primitive woodworking machines turned out a growing line of children's toys.

1939 to pitch in. One of his fellow participants in the work camps was my mother, Mary Raecher, daughter of a western New York dairy farmer, whom he had met at Cornell. They married shortly after the attack on Pearl Harbor.

Not all of the Greatest Generation fought in World War II. Of the conscientious objectors (COs) who refused to bear arms, twelve thousand did unpaid work of "national importance" in Civilian Public Service (CPS) camps, while six thousand went to prison. My father did both.

The urge to build a society that wouldn't lead to war propelled many COs and their families into intentional communities after the war. From my parents I heard many stories about those years: How my mother and another CO's wife kept the dairy going, milking twice a day while their husbands were at CPS camps. How my father rebelled at life in camp and went AWOL to milk the cows too. How Morris Mitchell reassured my father after Nagasaki that the feds wouldn't

Meanwhile, new families were welcomed and babies born. Child-rearing and education were hot issues. My parents sent my two older siblings to the one-room local school where Miss Ruby – not a pacifist – taught the three Rs with the help of a hickory switch. Unsurprisingly, some Macedonia parents wanted their own school. Personality conflicts arose and some families left, embittered. But the community also supported each other through the last days of an elder and the tragic deaths of two young children. When my parents' house burned down, they were welcomed into another member's home.

The endeavor had exceeded Morris Mitchell's original vision of economic uplift for the neighborhood and in 1948 he agreed to relinquish the project, deeding over the land to the young idealists on generous terms.

Foreground: Staughton and Alice, Alma Kneeland, Richard Mommsen, and Art Wiser, ca. 1956.
Background: Dave Dellinger, Staughton Lynd, and Robert Moses lead a protest march, August 6, 1965.

Macedonia hosted emissaries from the Bruderhof, then living as refugees in Paraguay due to their objection to war. The groups regarded each other highly, and in 1953 it looked like they might merge. But the Christian basis of the Bruderhof irked several agnostic Macedonians. Ultimately, half of Macedonia – three families – moved north to help found the first American Bruderhof, Woodcrest, in Rifton, New York. The break was amicable, with Macedonia's assets and debts divided in two, down to the woodworking machinery and the silverware. Each group's concern was that the other was well provided for. The woodworking business, Community Playthings, was to be carried on as a joint venture, with sales and manufacturing in both communities and a single mail-order catalog.

By June 1954, three families remained in Macedonia, determined to continue the community according to its original humanist ideals: Richard and Dorothy Mommsen with two children, Art and Mary Wiser with four, and Ivan and Alma Kneeland. Staughton and Alice Lynd visited in August 1954 and returned in November to stay.

～⁀～

Staughton Lynd's parents were Robert and Helen Lynd, authors of the influential 1929 sociological study *Middletown*. He and Alice met in 1950 at Harvard and Radcliffe and married within the year. In 1953 he was drafted, and, not wanting to fight, pursued basic training as a medic. But prompted by Senator Joe McCarthy's hearings, the Army was purging draftees suspected of communism. Based on purported Marxism in Staughton's college papers and his mother's professional career, he was discharged as "undesirable." Soon after, Staughton and Alice found their way to Macedonia.

The Lynds' daughter Barbara was born that first year. Hearths and tables were shared, and childcare, too. In a letter, my mother wrote, "We feel together the power of what has got hold of us – the naked truth which will be lived, which we cannot control."

It was a hardscrabble, simple life, as reflected in this poem Staughton wrote at the time:

Macedonia morning.
High on a pasture
In the dark,
Wool cap pulled above one ear,
Listening for cowbells.

Richard Mommsen returned home late one night with a donated wood planer in the back of his truck. The next morning, Ivan Kneeland chained the heavy machine to an overhead beam and drove the truck out from underneath, intending to lower the planer to the ground. The chain

Foreground: Staughton outside the Community Playthings shop, ca. 1956.
Background: Staughton being interviewed, August 6, 1965.

broke and the planer fell and cracked. Staughton was sure this would end the community, but no one seemed too upset. Stuff happened in Macedonia – accidents, illness, fires, friends leaving – but that didn't mean the end of their life together.

Staughton and Alice turned to Art and Mary for advice in the early years of their marriage. One evening in the dairy, the milking done, Staughton and Art talked about commitment. Staughton listened, amazed, as Art declared that if he had to choose between his calling and his marriage, he would choose Macedonia over Mary.

But competing commitments threatened the community. Business collaboration between the Bruderhof and Macedonia was bumpy. Religion, or its lack, kept derailing decisions. Finally one day Macedonia broke into crisis mode when Staughton chose to read aloud from *The Man Who Died* by D. H. Lawrence, a profane account of Christ's resurrection, at the common lunch table. Alma Kneeland, the sole churchgoer in the community, left the room in tears.

In Macedonia fashion, the members intended to talk things out and seek together for the truth. Their reading list spanned the Gospels, the Bhagavad Gita, and the Koran. Three months and seven chapters of Luke later, they were changed. Every Macedonia member was shaken. Someone drove forty-five minutes to the public phone in Clarkesville, across streams by ford and rickety bridge, and called the Bruderhof community at Woodcrest to beg that pastor J. Heinrich Arnold and his wife, Annemarie, drive down from New York.

Heinrich later described how Art "suggested that a group be formed around Jesus. People's faces became pale and shocked. Staughton was as though paralyzed. After a while he said, 'I feel lost. I feel an urge to put up the banner of truth anew and to call people around it. The truth remains even though people [he was looking at Art] become unfaithful.'"

When Staughton recalled this incident to me, he confirmed that it was the discussion in the dairy that he was remembering: "I did not take this as a legalistic commitment but as a personal

Foreground: The Lynds in 1955.
Background: Demonstrating for justice in Central America, ca. 1980.

promise that Art later broke." His mentor and dear friend had betrayed him.

In a few days all the members at Macedonia agreed to give the property to the Bruderhof and seek toward a membership commitment. Staughton's acquiescence testified to the depth of relationship the Lynds had found with their Macedonia companions.

The Lynds pitched in anew at Woodcrest. Staughton taught school, and their son Lee was born. But without a shared basis of faith it couldn't last. Staughton and Alice agreed to separate to let each seek his or her "best light." With their two children, Alice remained at the Bruderhof while Staughton spent nine "strange" months alone in New York City. Ultimately the family was reunited in the "hard, cold, capitalist world," as they called it. From then on, the couple was inseparable.

THE LYNDS' FEW SHORT YEARS at Macedonia and Woodcrest informed the rest of their lives. As Staughton wrote in *Living Inside Our Hope* (1997):

> The qualitatively different atmosphere of human relationships that we encountered at Macedonia has been our objective ever since. We found it again, to some extent, in the Southern civil rights movement, which sometimes called itself "a band of brothers and sisters standing in a circle of love"; in the practice of solidarity by rank-and-file workers; and in Latin American notions about "accompanying" one another in the search for "*el reino de Dios,*" the kingdom of God on earth. We found it in these other places because we were looking for it; because, after Macedonia, we knew it could happen.

Staughton's dissertation on democracy and class conflict in the Revolutionary War attracted Ivy League professorship offers. Instead he taught at Spelman College, a historically black school for women. Back in Georgia again, the Lynds sought out the civil rights movement. Staughton was invited by the Student Nonviolent Coordinating Committee (SNCC) to direct its Freedom Schools, a project concurrent with its 1964 Freedom Summer voter-registration drive.

In 1964 Yale offered Staughton an assistant professorship in history, and he taught there for three years. But his academic career came to an end when he visited Hanoi in 1966–67 on an unauthorized peace mission. Yale dropped him and academic offers elsewhere evaporated due to an FBI blacklist.

As the peace movement turned violent, Staughton deliberately gave up his leadership, and the Lynds moved to Chicago. Both became lawyers to more effectively help workers neglected by both corporations and the historic unions. They collected oral history "from the bottom up," recording meetings of steelworkers and nurses, electric linemen and retirees.

Foreground: Staughton and Alice married in 1951.
Background: Mug shot of Staughton, arrested on August 9, 1965.

In 1976, Staughton and Alice moved to Youngstown, Ohio, where prisons had replaced the steel mills. "Accompanying" the powerless led them to public defender work, to Central America, and to Palestine. After a prison riot and standoff at nearby Lucasville in 1993, several prisoners were arbitrarily convicted of the murder of a guard. The Lynds came to their defense and found themselves helping death-row inmates, to whom they came to be known as Scrapper and Mama Bear.

Soon Mama Bear was behind bars herself, in contempt of court: Alice had a prison client who confessed to a murder committed during the uprising. The confession was protected under attorney-client privilege, but other lawyers exploited it and subpoenaed Alice to testify. As a Quaker, she could not participate in actions that would put anyone on death row, and refused to provide "snitch testimony." She was prepared to face prison indefinitely – and then her client released his privilege and authorized her to testify. He couldn't stand the thought of his plucky seventy-five-year-old lawyer incarcerated.

Staughton went to fetch Alice from jail. As he entered through the crowd of supporters he heard his wife singing. She had kept her spirits up with the old Quaker hymn "How Can I Keep from Singing" – "no storm can shake my inmost calm while to that rock I'm clinging" – and "Dona Nobis Pacem."

The Lynds wrote and edited many books, starting with Staughton's *Nonviolence in America* (1966) and including Alice's *We Won't Go* (1968). *Rank and File*, drawn from the workers' oral histories they assembled, went through four editions.

They also kept in touch with their old friends at the Bruderhof. The other former Macedonians were believers now, and Staughton a self-styled existentialist. Old differences continued to resurface, but they never stopped corresponding.

⌒⌒

In early 2015 my wife, Maureen, and I were driving through Niles, Ohio, and enjoyed Staughton and Alice's hospitality at their modest ranch house, outfitted with hand-me-down appliances and decades' worth of activist memorabilia. The Lynds welcomed us with true Macedonia camaraderie. On the kitchen table was an artifact of our childhood, a Woodcrest songbook. The corners of its antique mimeographed pages were worn round by use. Staughton and Alice wanted to sing the old songs together.

Staughton once told me, "I try to live by Matthew 25 to the extent that I am able to do so." He understood that fundamentally everyone's calling is to love the hungry, the sick, the stranger, the prisoner. He was heartened to see that the vision that had taken root in him on those frosty mornings on Georgia hillsides and that led him to decades of fruitful antiwar, civil rights, and labor activism was continuing to bear fruit in other lives, like mine, indelibly shaped by the ventured dared at Macedonia. Planers can break and houses burn. But along Shoal Creek my mother's daffodils have spread into the woods from her burned-down threshold. They bloom again every spring. ⤳

Foreground: Staughton and Alice at their wedding in 1951.
Background: Celebrating sixty-eight years of marriage in 2019.

Photograph by Václav Mach. Used by permission.

World Within

Cattai Wetlands

You walk a zone of woodland, dense
And shadow-fretted, a slow arc,
And, you imagine, a circumference
Of she-oak, paperbark,

That must eventually complete
Its promise, an unbroken ring,
Surrounding? You proceed on unrushed feet,
Watching and listening.

But no. You happen on a break,
From which, unsigned, a pathway leads,
Right-angled to the course you thought to take,
To water grasses, reeds,

And falling open, like the gap
Within the fabric of the world
Mystics bear witness to, though on no map,
Before your eyes unfurled,

A lake of waterlilies, spread
At the day's heart, to keep the day.
The floating light of noon, distributed
And clinging to delay

What used to pass for time, makes clear
The shallows at your feet, and adds
Lustres that intermittently appear
Among the lily pads.

A fantail seems to pause and flare,
A rufous snapshot on the sky,
And like a jewel fastened to midair,
Hovers a dragonfly.

Watching the light stretched membrane-still,
Midday on hold, you acquiesce,
And feel a—what?—an empty presence fill
Your unclaimed consciousness.

Black swans in languid ones and twos
Continually patrol their realm,
Like stewards, bending down to strain the ooze
Or from the surface film

Skim slime and delicately sift
Blown smuts of matter that begrime
The sheen, as though the air in tainted drift
Shed the rank spores of time.

STEPHEN EDGAR

Photograph: Václav Mach,
Cattai Wetlands, 2018.

Tim Keller: New York's Pastor

The quintessential pastor of Manhattan
held the doors open to everyone in need of the gospel.

SUSANNAH BLACK ROBERTS

I N THE DAYS AFTER 9/11, New Yorkers read in the *Times* that Jerry Falwell had told them they deserved it. They were God's enemies, and, presumably, Falwell's too.

The Sunday before 9/11, Redeemer Presbyterian Church's weekly attendance hovered at 2,800, after two decades of slow but steady growth. On September 16, 5,400 people attended a service. Around 800 new members were added to the rolls in the weeks afterward.

The sermon Tim Keller had planned for that Sunday had been on Jonah – the prophet who, sent to a great and sinful city, attempts to avoid going at all costs, because he is so irritated at the prospect that God loves it and its people and is eager to forgive them. Keller scrapped that one. He preached that Sunday instead on the raising of Lazarus.

When Jesus reaches the house of his friends Mary and Martha and finds that their brother Lazarus is dead, he weeps. "When somebody says to me, 'I don't know that God cares about our suffering, I don't know that God cares about it at all,' I say, 'Yes, he does,'" said Keller from the pulpit that morning to the sea of new faces, people who did not ordinarily go to church at all.

They say, "How do you know?" Well, I'll tell you something. If I was in any other religion I wouldn't know what to say. But what I can say is: the proof is he was willing to suffer himself. I don't know why he hasn't ended suffering and evil by now, but the fact that he was willing to be involved

and he himself got involved . . . [shows that] he is not remote.

Jesus was not absent from New York that Sunday.

Ten years after 9/11, polling revealed that attendance at evangelical churches in the city had tripled. According to Colin Hansen's biography of Keller, between 1989 and 2019 the number of Manhattan residents attending such churches grew from nine thousand to over eighty thousand.

Keller's wife, Kathy, gives credit for this where it is, primarily, due. "You want to know how to plant a successful church? Find out where God is beginning a revival, and move there the month before."

Keller did not have a burning ambition to be accepted by the people of New York when he and Kathy moved there from rural Virginia in 1989. This was helpful in shaping him into someone able to challenge New Yorkers as well as contextualize the gospel for them.

"It's surprising that so many educated twenty- and thirty-somethings would attend a church that teaches against sex outside marriage," Kathy Keller once said to a journalist, who laughed: "Yes, that *would* be surprising."

"No," said Kathy, "I'm saying that's what we actually teach."

Keller ministered to secular New Yorkers, but he ministered as well to many who were raised evangelical outside the city and moved there after college: those who, one might think, are primed to shed their Christianity, finding that it can't coexist with their love of the city's culture or their

Susannah Black Roberts is a senior editor of Plough.

city-sized ambition (in New York these things are often fused.)

When these people started going to Redeemer, they watched *Babette's Feast*, because Keller couldn't really go for very long without recommending it. The story is of a great Parisian chef who, after spending years serving a pair of sisters in a remote, pious village in Jutland, wins the lottery and spends her winnings on a feast that overcomes the villagers' dour asceticism.

Evangelicals who saw the film experienced themselves as the ones who had lived lives of duty, and who were now given permission to pursue beauty. They found in this the gospel of grace: Jesus pouring out his riches, inviting them to taste and see that the Lord is good, and also letting them know that they could get involved in all kinds of pursuits of excellence and beauty. They were encouraged, at Redeemer, to be actors, singers, musicians, artists, or filmmakers. Redeemer's urban take on the creation mandate told them that much of what they'd been raised to think was questionable because it was not evangelism might be worthwhile in itself.

When those raised in New York, or imbued in its culture, come to Redeemer, they do not need to be told that art and beauty and excellence are worthwhile in themselves; they have been raised on that gospel. And if they are succeeding in New York, they are succeeding on its terms. But if they are succeeding in New York, and if they have any imagination at all, they know that isn't enough.

They also watch *Babette's Feast*. There's a scene at the end, after the feast is over, when all that remains are dirty dishes. In Isak Dinesen's original book version, the line of dialogue between Babette and one of the sisters says, "'I feel, Babette, that this is not the end. In Paradise you will be the great artist that God meant you to be! Ah!' she added, the tears streaming down her cheeks, 'Ah, how you will enchant the angels!'"

If Christ had not been raised, beauty would be merely a defiant flame in the eternal dark. The end would simply be the end of the song, the end of the Broadway run, the dirty dishes at the end of the meal.

Keller's ministry was aimed at both Babette and the two sisters.

The Jutlanders needed the urban artist Babette to remind them of the goodness of God as seen in his world and in the work of human hands. Babette desperately needed the word that the sisters knew, to learn that goodness was aimed at something, that it is an ethical and not just an aesthetic beauty, that in the gospel beauty and holiness meet and kiss.

Evangelicals leaving home for New York needed something like Keller's ministry to prevent them from leaving the faith. Secular New Yorkers needed a word from outside their city – from the New Jerusalem – to give them life.

Keller gave his New York congregation a new City to love, a City that draws together red and blue, urban and rural, Americans and those half a world away. It is the love of this City that will ultimately overcome all enmity. It is in this City that we find our peace.

Brian Kershisnik, *Divine Intervention*, oil on canvas, 2016

What Is Time For?

ZENA HITZ

Everyone is too busy. How would we spend our time if we weren't?

IN HIS *CONFESSIONS*, Saint Augustine describes a fascinating moment in his conversion to the Christian faith. At the time, he was a successful teacher of rhetoric in Milan, living with his longtime concubine and their son. He had a group of close friends and was breaking away from the Manichaeans, the gnostic cult he had spent many years with, studying and teaching. Overwhelmed by the limits of human knowledge, he was increasingly skeptical that anyone could come to know the truth about how to live. He oscillated back and forth between skepticism that anything certain could be known and his budding interest in the Christian faith, the latter nurtured by hearing the preaching of Ambrose, bishop of Milan. He describes his internal dialogue at the time:

> But where can truth be sought? *When* can it be sought? Ambrose has no time. There is no time for reading. Where should we look for the

books that we need? Where and when can we obtain them? From whom can we borrow them? Fixed times must be kept free, hours appointed, for the health of the soul. Great hope has been aroused. . . . Why do we hesitate to knock at the door which opens the way to all the rest? Our pupils occupy the mornings; what should we do with the remaining hours? Why do we not investigate our problem? But then when should we go to pay respects to our more influential friends, whose patronage we need? When are we to prepare what our students are paying for? When are we to refresh ourselves by allowing the mind to relax from the tension of anxieties?[1]

Augustine's language can be lofty and remote. But here is one of his great human moments. He wants to know how to live. He is not worried about discovering a truth that might spoil his career or require him to leave his concubine. Really! He doesn't have time, that's all – he's too busy, between his students and his patrons, oh, and Ambrose is too busy too. Everyone's too busy. He doesn't have time to read. Besides, he doesn't have time to get the books. Too bad for Augustine – he can't figure out the best way to live. He's too busy.

Earlier in the same section of the *Confessions*, Augustine describes how busy Ambrose is. Ambrose is busy. Bishops of that time were expected to adjudicate disputes between members of their flock, an endless and demanding task. The life of a bishop was so hectic, in fact, that later in life, after he had become Catholic, Augustine would do almost anything to avoid being appointed one. The historian Peter Brown describes him as going from town to town in Africa, carefully avoiding any occasion in which he might be appointed bishop by acclamation. Alas, he was tricked: in Hippo he found himself

at a liturgy that became his election as bishop. Tears poured down his face as he realized his life of philosophical leisure was over.

Yet Augustine describes with reverence what Ambrose does in the brief moments in which he does not have an appointment. He reads silently. He does not steal away to a quiet place. Ambrose just sits and reads in the midst of his busyness, passing his eyes over the page.

I could not put the questions I wanted to put to him as I wished to do. I was excluded from his ear and from his mouth by crowds of men with arbitrations to submit to him, to whose frailties he ministered. When he was not with them, which was a very brief period of time, he restored either his body with necessary food or his mind by reading. When he was reading, his eyes ran over the page and his heart perceived the sense, but his voice and tongue were silent. He did not restrict access to anyone coming in, nor was it customary even for a visitor to be announced. Very often when we were there, we saw him silently reading and never otherwise. After sitting for a long time in silence (for who would dare to burden him in such intent concentration?) we used to go away. We supposed that in the brief time he could find for his mind's refreshment, free from the hubbub of other people's troubles, he would not want to be invited to consider another problem.[2]

Ambrose has chosen to use his spare snatches of time to return within himself, to become an island of stillness. His reading, certainly, is an example of *leisure*.

WHAT IS LEISURE, and why is it necessary for human beings? The leisure that I am interested in is not the first thing you may imagine: bingeing Netflix on the

1. Augustine, *Confessions*, trans. Henry Chadwick (Oxford: Oxford University Press, 2009), 104 (6.11.18).

2. Augustine, *Confessions*, 92–3 (6.3.3).

Zena Hitz is a tutor at St. John's College and the author of Lost in Thought: The Hidden Pleasures of an Intellectual Life *(2020) and* A Philosopher Looks at the Religious Life *(2023).*

couch, lounging at the beach, attending a festive party with friends, or launching yourself from the largest human catapult for the thrill of it. The leisure that is necessary for human beings is not just a break from real life, a place where we rest and restore ourselves in order to go back to work. What we are after is a state that looks like the culmination of a life.

Let's pause and ask ourselves: What parts of our lives seem to be the culminating parts, the days or hours or minutes where we are living life most fully? When do you stop counting the time and become entirely present to what you are doing? What sorts of activities are you engaged in when this takes place?

We do many things instrumentally, for the sake of something else: eat breakfast to calm hunger pains, exercise to stay healthy, work for money. Other things we do for pleasure: play cards, go for hikes, read, or build model airplanes. Some things evidently both are instrumental and bring us delight: we work for money, but sometimes also for the love of our work; we fish to eat, but also for the sport of it.

We have many goals, but certain goals have an ordering effect on others. We either choose our career to permit leisure time with our family, or we choose to minimize familial obligations to allow free upward growth in our career. Our ultimate end – family in the first case, success in the second – frames and structures our other pursuits. We trade a freer schedule for more money or sacrifice a higher salary for more time to pursue our heart's desire. The structuring effect of some goals over others suggests that we have a basic orientation, determined by our ultimate end, the goal that structures all our other choices. Such a goal is our highest good, whether we have chosen it as such, or whether it has grown haphazardly out of inward or social pressures. That highest good or ultimate end might be wealth, status, family life, community service, enjoyment of the natural world, knowledge of God, writing novels,

What parts of our lives seem to be the culminating parts, the days or hours or minutes where we are living life most fully? When do you stop counting the time and become entirely present to what you are doing?

Brian Kershisnik, *Something About Young Trees*, oil on canvas, 2017.

or even the pursuit of mathematical truth.

We may not know what in the soup of our desires matters most to us. Often we discover it in times of trial or crisis: a difficult choice at work, a family member in a hospital bed – in other words, when we face sickness, poverty, or moral compromise.

What would happen if we tried to organize our lives around merely instrumental pursuits? We are not likely to order our lives around grocery shopping or paying taxes. But what about earning money? If I pack my swim bag, put on shoes, get my keys, and drive my car to the pool, only to find it closed, my goal of swimming is frustrated, and my string of actions is in vain. Suppose the pool is open and I get to swim: Why do I do it? I swim for the sake of health. I want to be healthy so I can work. I work for the sake of money. And the money is for the sake of food, drink, housing, recreation, and exercise – all of which make it possible for me to work.

I have described a life of utter futility. If I work for the sake of money, spending money on basic necessities, and if my life is organized around working, my life is a pointless spiral of work for the sake of work. It is like buying ice cream, immediately selling it for cash, and then spending the proceeds on ice cream (which one sells once again, and so on). It is just as tragic as working for money and getting crushed by a falling anvil on the way to cash the paycheck. For this reason Aristotle argued that there must be some activity or activities beyond work – leisure, for the sake of which we work and without which our work is in vain. Leisure is not merely recreation, which we might undertake for the sake of work – to relax or rest before beginning to labor anew. It is an activity or set of activities that could count as the culmination of all our endeavors. For Aristotle, only contemplation could be ultimately satisfying in this way: the activity of seeing and understanding and savoring the world as it is.

> *For Aristotle, only contemplation could be ultimately satisfying in this way: the activity of seeing and understanding and savoring the world as it is.*

Brian Kershisnik, *She Reads*, oil on panel, 2006.

WHAT DOES CONTEMPLATIVE LEISURE look like in real life? I've collected a few examples. Renée, heroine of the French art-house film *The Hedgehog*, is the concierge of a wealthy apartment building in Paris. Her work is humble – cleaning, taking mail, organizing the workmen. But her real life is elsewhere – in a hidden room behind her kitchen, where she reads philosophy, literature, and the classics.

Renée echoes a similar figure in an earlier film, *Ali: Fear Eats the Soul*, by the German director Rainer Werner Fassbinder. Emmi is a middle-aged cleaning lady at the bottom of the social barrel. To the horror of her xenophobic children and neighbors, she falls in love with a younger Moroccan guest worker. They make a strange couple, crossing age groups and races. But they find a refuge that two people sometimes find, a space away from demeaning judgments, where they contemplate in one another their simple, vulnerable humanity. In one scene, they sit alone at an outdoor café, surrounded by fallen autumn leaves, holding hands and gazing into each other's eyes. This film is more tragic than *The Hedgehog*, since the protagonists rely on each other for their refuge, and since they carry within themselves the expectations from their social world – expectations which destroy their relationship.

The leisured contemplation in loving relationships is worth mentioning, since it is the type most commonly recognized and valued today. But there is also the more traditional, intellectual form of leisure: Renée sequestered in her room reading, cat curled at her feet. Consider the medieval and Renaissance paintings of Mary at the Annunciation. These images, drawing on early Christian writers, often picture Mary reading a book. Here is Ambrose:

> She, when the angel entered, was found at home in privacy, without a companion, that no one might interrupt her attention or disturb her; and she did not desire any women as companions, who had the companionship of good thoughts. Moreover, she seemed to herself to be less alone when she was alone. For how should she be alone, who had with her so many books, so many archangels, so many prophets?[3]

Images of study and intellectual life as a leisured refuge are older than Christianity: Plato describes his teacher Socrates as lost in thought, standing all dressed up on the threshold of a dinner party, having forgotten where he is. The great mathematician Archimedes was by legend so lost in his theorems that he did not notice the Romans invading his city and was killed by a Roman soldier when he insisted on finishing his proof before going to the Roman official who had summoned him. Later writers gave him last words: "Don't disturb my circles."

Nor are these images only in fiction or legend or ancient tradition. Albert Einstein was a failure as a graduate student in physics and could not get an academic job. He found work as a patent clerk; it was in the patent office, in his spare time, that he wrote the extraordinary papers on the photoelectric effect and Brownian movement that changed the face of the mathematical study of nature. He called the patent office "that worldly cloister where I hatched all my most beautiful ideas."

Prisoners have been among the most splendid exemplars of leisure. The Russian dissident Irina Ratushinskaya describes prisoners in transport passing poetry to one another, written on scraps of paper. Ratushinskaya herself, during her own imprisonment in Siberia, scratched poems onto soap bars with matchsticks. Once she had memorized them, she washed them away. Later she wrote them out on cigarette paper to be smuggled to the West.[4] Irina Dumitrescu writes of a Romanian officer imprisoned in Siberia who

3. Ambrose, *Concerning Virginity*, trans. H. de Romestin, E. de Romestin and H. T. F. Duckworth, in *Nicene and Post-Nicene Fathers, Second Series*, Vol. 10, ed. Philip Schaff and Henry Wace (Buffalo, NY: Christian Literature, 1896).
4. Irina Ratushinskaya, *Grey Is the Color of Hope*, trans. Alyona Kojevnikov (New York: Knopf, 1988), 75.

wrote out poems he had memorized in school with ink that he made out of blackberries. Other Romanian prisoners tapped poetry in Morse code through the walls of the prison, or taught each other languages in silence, with letters coded by knots on a piece of string.

What explains the power of these examples? I think it is because they show the dignity of human beings, the fact that a human being is not reducible to his or her social uses. The forcible diminishment of the prisoners is an attempt at thought control, to make them think or speak as authorities would like them to. Likewise, the commonplace diminishment of working people such as building supervisors or cleaning ladies does not suppress the splendor of a human being, or it does so only superficially. Mary, after all, is an unwed teenage mother. Her prayerful and studious solitude suggests a dignity beyond the social uses set for young women of her era: sexual pleasure, the extension of clans and bloodlines. We see all these people choosing forms of leisure – thinking, study, prayer, love – in the face of opposition, resistance, or outright hostility.

These are, however, exceptional human beings. Sometimes, hostile circumstances make leisure very difficult or even impossible. Jack London tells the semiautobiographical tale of Martin Eden in his novel by that name. Martin is working class but is giving himself an intensive education through reading and study. However, he has to eat, and at some point he takes the only job he can find, working in a laundry for fifteen-hour days, six days a week. This type of work is so exhausting that after only a week, he is unable to read. After several weeks, he is unable to think and takes refuge in cheap pleasures.

Likewise, consider the situation of the Amazon warehouse worker, as described by journalist James Bloodworth.[5] Thanks to the choices of their company executives, the workers are hired

The example of restless, workaholic Augustine is important. It is not true that he doesn't have time. The fact is he, like us, is of two minds about leisure. He, like us, is afraid of it.

5. James Bloodworth, *Hired: Six Months Undercover in Low-Wage Britain* (London: Atlantic Books, 2018).

Brian Kershisnik, *Disheveled Saint*, oil on paper, 2001.

by a temp company, which monitors their every move with surveillance bracelets, penalizes them for bathroom breaks or illness, holds out the promise of rewards that never materialize, changes schedules capriciously, docks their pay, sometimes by mistake, and in general makes workers so riven with anxiety and exhausted by overwork that cheap pleasures become enormously attractive, even to those to whom they had not been previously. So the capacity for leisure can be made more difficult, or even impossible, by circumstances.

Now, however, we face a puzzle. If leisure is what our lives aim at, how could we fail to achieve it – we, that is, who are not deprived by circumstances? What are the obstacles in us to attaining our highest good? How is it that we ourselves, through our own choices, diminish our dignity?

The example of restless, workaholic Augustine is important. It is not true that he doesn't have time. The fact is he, like us, is of two minds about leisure. He wants it and he doesn't want it. He's committed to other things: his job, his students, his patrons, his rest, and his social advancement above all. That is worth dwelling on for a moment. But there is a deeper problem: It's not just that he doesn't want to make sacrifices; he is actively avoiding leisure. He, like us, is afraid of it.

Work in itself, of course, can be a good thing. It is the way that we serve our communities. That is true if we work at a business that supplies something that people need to live; or if we work to raise our children; or if we work as teachers, doctors, lawyers, electricians, garbage collectors, health care aides, and so on.

Yet good things, as we know from everyday experience, are not always good. Food is a good thing, until we overeat. Sex is a good thing, but we can use it in demeaning or dehumanizing or otherwise harmful ways. I think it may already be clear how we misuse work. After all, how many of us really think of it as service, rather than as a vehicle for money or status? How many of us are genuinely open to serving our communities however we are most needed, even if serving that need doesn't pay much or has a low social status – if, for instance, it will be scorned by people we talk to on airplanes?

Nowhere are our true feelings about work clearer than in the growth of jobs which pay well and offer high status, but which have little to no social value. Sociologist David Graeber calls them bullshit jobs.[6] (It is difficult to find a non-profane word that combines the pointlessness of these jobs with the necessary deception they involve.) Bullshit jobs are both pointless and require pretending that they are not pointless. One example: being a subcontractor to a subcontractor to the military, whose job it is to drive long distances to move furniture from one room to another. More poignant is the story of the man hired to patch a problem that the higher authorities in the company do not want fixed. He is literally paid – and paid well – to do nothing. He starts out reading novels, then starts drinking at work and taking phony work trips, trying to get himself fired. Finally, he tries to resign and gets offered a raise. His job is a necessary pretense for his superiors – they cannot let him go. What is fascinating about the stories Graeber collects is how deeply unhappy these workers are, people who have money and status without having to work for it. It seems that their hearts long for real work, for service, for connection with their communities.

We think of American culture – a culture shared with much of Western Europe – as a culture that values work. But it is not in fact work that we value. What we value is money and status, no matter the cost in other human goods. It is its connection with money and with status that allows work to become addictive or compulsive. After all, remember Augustine, who finds himself plenty busy, always with an end of social advancement. But let's also remember Ambrose. He has

6. David Graeber, *Bullshit Jobs* (New York: Simon and Schuster, 2018).

more work than anybody, but he knows how to use his breaks. His leisure shows us what he cares about most; it shows both why his work matters and why it doesn't matter.

We are not only distracted from leisure by conflicting desires for social advancement. We also fear it and resist it from inside. Our resistance to it is both powerful and devious. We can see this in the deterioration of professions or vocations strictly dedicated to leisure. For example, one could join a monastery and live obsessed with high liturgical achievements such as the perfect performance of the best music. Or one could try to work one's way up whatever social hierarchy may exist there – to be choir director, cellarer, abbot. Or one could try to be a monk or nun for

> *We seek out distractions in order to hide from this terrifying emptiness that can only be filled with God.*

the world, dedicating one's time to winning new vocations or publicity for religious life. None of these objectives is bad in itself, but their pursuit can eat away at one's humanity. A person can live in a monastery, under vows of poverty, chastity, and obedience, and still nurture the heart of a politician or social climber.

Likewise, any professor can tell you that despite ancient tradition, true leisure in academia is hard to come by. At the bottom end, hapless adjuncts manage large classes in which often virtually no learning takes place. Their grading burden is such that time for real thinking is rare. At the top end, we find a ruthless pursuit of arcane forms of status. The rush for prestige, for producing articles or books that make an impression, for networking, for climbing up the institutional ladder, makes much of academic life no more

leisurely than the average Fortune 500 company.

Other examples of leisurely activity are no less fragile than monastic life or academic life. A life outdoors can be overtaken by advocacy or forms of competition; family life can be rotted through with a frenetic, soul-destroying race for achievement.

Leisure requires cultivation – cultivation of habits and of communities that help to form habits. The pursuit of leisure requires this effort because we resist it. Augustine does not only desire social advancement – he is also afraid of leisure itself. What is Augustine afraid of? What is it *in us* that flees from leisure? It is, simply speaking, our own emptiness. Saint John of the Cross describes the human soul as made up of great caverns, caverns constituted by our senses and their emptiness constituted by their necessary passivity, receptivity, susceptibility. We seek out distractions in order to hide from this terrifying emptiness that can only be filled with God. The emptiness is our dependence on what comes from the outside, our need to wait for God to act. This dependence and this need are objectively terrifying. What will come? An earthquake? Cancer? Joblessness? More to the point: What will we find in ourselves? That we love status and money more than we thought we did? That we don't know ourselves, or God, or what matters in our lives?

Leisure turns out to be an *interior discipline*. It is not enough to simply choose a central life activity that is intrinsically leisurely. One must recognize the good of leisure and seek it out. Moreover, leisure might require *sacrifice*. A less lucrative job might permit more time with one's family. A less prestigious academic post might permit a greater focus on studying and contemplative teaching. The examples of Ambrose, Renée, and Ratushinskaya show, I hope, that leisure is worth the cost, and that it is possible. ⤳

This is a chapter from Plough's *forthcoming book* The Liberating Arts: Why We Need Liberal Arts Education *(September 2023). See page 100.*

PLOUGH BOOKLIST

Subscribers 30% discount: use code **PQ30** at checkout.

Members 50% discount: call for code or check your members-only newsletter. Plough Members automatically get new Plough books. Learn more at *plough.com/members*.

When Enemies Threaten

Why Forgive?

Johann Christoph Arnold

In *Why Forgive?* Arnold lets the untidy experiences of ordinary people speak for themselves – people who have earned the right to talk about forgiving. Some of these stories deal with violent crime, betrayal, abuse, hate, gang warfare, and genocide. Others address everyday hurts: the wounds caused by backbiting, gossip, conflicts in the home, and tensions in the workplace. This book also tackles what can be the biggest challenge: forgiving ourselves.

Softcover, 232 pages, ~~$12.00~~ **$8.40 with subscriber discount**

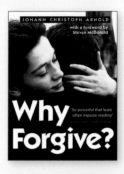

From Red Earth

A Rwandan Story of Healing and Forgiveness

Denise Uwimana

At the height of the genocide, as men with bloody machetes ransacked her home, Denise Uwimana gave birth to her third son. With the unlikely help of Hutu Good Samaritans, she and her children survived. Her husband and other family members were not as lucky. She has devoted the rest of her life to restoring her country by empowering other genocide widows to band together, tell their stories, find healing, and rebuild their lives.

Softcover, 232 pages, ~~$18.00~~ **$12.60 with subscriber discount**

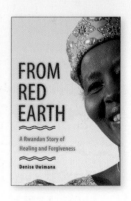

Mandela and the General

John Carlin, Oriol Malet (artist)

As the first post-apartheid elections approach in 1994, with South African blacks poised to take power, the nation's whites fear reprisal. Mandela knows that he can't avert a bloodbath on his own. He will have to count on his archenemy, General Constand Viljoen, former chief of apartheid South Africa's military. Throughout those historic months, the two men meet in secret. Can they trust each other? Can they keep their followers and radical fringe elements from acts of violence? The mettle of these two men will determine the future of a nation.

Jon Lee Anderson: A timely reminder of the value of human empathy as a tool in political confrontation.

Softcover, 112 pages, ~~$19.95~~ **$13.96 with subscriber discount**

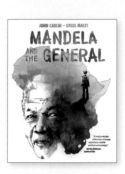

New Releases

The Liberating Arts
Why We Need Liberal Arts Education
Edited by Jeffrey Bilbro, Jessica Hooten Wilson, and David Henreckson

Why would anyone study the liberal arts? It's no secret that the liberal arts have fallen out of favor and are struggling to prove their relevance. They are accused of being a waste of time, racist, liberal, elitist, out of touch, and a bad career investment.

A new cohort of educators isn't taking this lying down. They realize they need to reimagine and rearticulate what a liberal arts education is for, and what it might look like in today's world.

John Baskin, editor, *Harper's*: In this lucid and inspiring volume, a diverse group of thinkers dispel entrenched falsehoods about the irrelevance, injustice, or uselessness of the liberal arts and remind us that nothing is more fundamental to preparing citizens to live in a pluralistic society attempting to balance the values of justice, equality, and community.
Softcover, 224 pages, ~~$18.00~~ **$12.60 with subscriber discount**

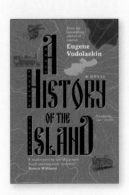

A History of the Island
A Novel
Eugene Vodolazkin
Translated by Lisa C. Hayden

Monks devious and devout – and an age-defying royal pair – chronicle the history of their fictional island in this witty critique of Western civilization and the idea of history itself.

Eugene Vodolazkin, internationally acclaimed novelist and scholar of medieval literature, returns with a satirical parable about European history, the myth of progress, and the futility of war. His chroniclers dutifully narrate events they witness: quests for power, betrayals, civil wars, plagues, droughts, invasions, and revolutions. But at least one monk simultaneously drafts and hides a "true" history, to be discovered centuries later. Vodolazkin recasts history in all its hubris and horror, while finding the humor in its absurdity.

Gary Saul Morson, *New York Review of Books*: Eugene Vodolazkin has emerged in the eyes of many as the most important living Russian writer.

Rowan Williams: A masterpiece by one of Europe's finest contemporary novelists.
Hardcover, 320 pages, ~~$26.95~~ **$18.87 with subscriber discount**

By Water
The Felix Manz Story
Jason Landsel, Sankha Banerjee, and Richard Mommsen

Five hundred years ago, in an age marked by war, plague, inequality, and religious coercion, there were people across Europe who dared to imagine a society of sharing, peace, and freedom of conscience. These radicals were executed by the thousands – by water, by fire, and by sword. Their story comes to life in this graphic novel, the first in a series that dramatically recreates a little-known chapter in the history of the Reformation.
Softcover, 144 pages, ~~$19.95~~ **$13.96 with subscriber discount**

The Monsignor versus the Fascists

In and around the Vatican, Hugh O'Flaherty organized a daring network to hide Jews and escaping prisoners of war.

MAUREEN SWINGER

TWO MEN CLAD in a monsignor's signature black and scarlet glided slowly across the Piazza di Circo Neoniani, past the Swiss Guard and the Italian gendarmes, murmuring devoutly and certainly not turning their heads to scout for Gestapo soldiers. "Mind now, me boy, walk slowly . . . none of that parade ground strut!

Keep your head bowed, and pray all the time. If you don't know any prayers, keep your lips moving anyway!" Monsignor Hugh O'Flaherty had lent his spare cassock, and now was lending his urgent advice to Major Sam Derry of the British Royal Artillery, thrice-escaped prisoner of war and now another O'Flaherty conspirator.

A German Panzer tank in front of the Altare della Patria in Rome, February 1944.

Hugh O'Flaherty's childhood was spent in Killarney, Ireland. Hearing a distinct call to the priesthood, he was worried about telling his father, knowing the state of the family finances. So he employed his sister Bride to break the news. Their father's response: "I would sell the house to make a priest of him."

O'Flaherty enrolled at the Jesuits' Mungret College near Limerick, where by all accounts he did well in his studies, but better at golf, boxing, handball, and hurling. Posted to Rome in 1922, just as Mussolini was rising to power, he was ordained in 1925 and continued his studies. Drawn into Vatican service, his life as a diplomat took

him to Egypt, then Haiti and Santo Domingo, then Czechoslovakia.

By 1938 he was recalled again to Rome, to an appointment in the Sacred Congregation of the Holy Office: what was once the Inquisition. Now he was mingling with Roman society, invited to galas and operas. He joined the Rome Golf Club, which earned him the moniker "the golfing priest."

Declaring allegiance to the Axis Powers in June 1940, Mussolini sent shock waves through Italy; with armies and armaments depleted after years of conflict in Africa and Albania, the country was not united behind their leader's actions. But war was at their doorstep anyway.

O'Flaherty's office was assigned the duty of visiting thousands of Allied prisoners of war in camps scattered across northern Italy, to verify fair treatment. He took down names and details, then, back in Rome, had them broadcast over the Radio Vatican to notify next of kin that their relatives were alive.

On his visits to the camps, he brought Red Cross parcels, prayer books, and cigarettes, and lobbied to increase the number of doctors and chaplains available. Eventually these actions got him removed from the job, though not before he filed complaints about two commanders who were dealing out especially cruel treatment to prisoners. His visits had also served another purpose; his name and face were recognized by many who later escaped to Rome.

And then came a new task: not, this time, one to which he was officially assigned, except perhaps by Providence.

O'Flaherty was lodged at the German College. Though not within the confines of the Vatican, it was Vatican property and therefore under its protection of neutrality, immune from searches by Mussolini's men and, later, the Gestapo.

It started small. Jewish families and others endangered by the regime were quietly routed first to O'Flaherty's lodgings, then to convents and hostels run by trusted acquaintances. Soon

A soldier sits at the entrance to the Vatican, 1944. Photograph by John Alden Rusch Jr.

POW camp escapees started showing up in St. Peter's Square, begging for sanctuary. When the Allies invaded Sicily, Mussolini's regime toppled and Italy surrendered in July 1943; the trickle of escapees became a flood, as the Third Reich moved south to claim the camps and ship the prisoners north.

Pope Pius XII's predecessor had engineered a blanket of neutrality over the Vatican and its properties, but, not wishing to compromise his diplomatic standing, Pius refused to lift the blanket in order to give sanctuary to refugees. The Swiss Guard were told to refuse entry to all seeking refuge in the city-state.

The pope likely knew about O'Flaherty's rapidly branching covert pipeline, but he never shut it down. The priest was called in at one point. He never revealed what was said to him.

Whatever it was, O'Flaherty interpreted it as, "Be more sneaky." From his post of observation on the steps of St. Peter's Square, he intercepted each small party of sanctuary seekers before they reached the Swiss Guard, and coworkers helped scatter them throughout the city in safe houses. They managed to hide people in an Italian police barracks for months. Another hideout was directly adjacent to the Rome SS headquarters. Some of the squad impersonated priests, soldiers, and delivery men. Others smuggled fugitives under loads of cabbages destined for German commissaries. One group "borrowed" the uniform of the Swiss Guard and tagged along at the end of the midnight changing-of-the-guard, then kept on marching. Many of the city's trolley-car operators were in on the operation.

All who joined the venture knew there was someone pulling the network together. He was known to them as Golf (not the most original code name, but it held). Some of the most stalwart members were escapees. One early addition to the ranks was Princess Nini Pallavicini, of one of Rome's noble families, whose vocal disapproval of Mussolini's government had brought her under

suspicion. When the police traced illegal radio broadcasts to Nini's palazzo, she escaped the raid by jumping out of a window. O'Flaherty tucked her away in the German College, where she ran a successful document-forging operation for the remainder of the war.

By November 1943, the nameless organization had hidden away over a thousand persons. After safe cover, the most urgent need was money. O'Flaherty approached D'Arcy Osborne, a golfing acquaintance and the twelfth Duke of Leeds and British Minister to the Holy See.

Osborne turned him down; he knew he was being watched. From Osborne's journal: "While guests of the pope, we are at the same time to some extent prisoners of the Italian government."

Shortly thereafter, the minister privately contacted O'Flaherty to assure him of as much financial support as he personally was able to secure. Even better, he offered the services of his butler, John May, whom O'Flaherty was to describe as "indispensable, a genius, the most

Monsignor Hugh O'Flaherty in Haiti.

magnificent scrounger I have ever come across." Discreet and completely loyal, May ran strategies from within the British ambassador's offices inside the Vatican.

Osborne – code name Mount – threw his untraceable resources at the organization throughout the duration of the war. Upon meeting Major Sam Derry at a social function (Derry still helpfully disguised as a monsignor), Osborne approved his addition to the team; subsequently Derry took on much of the communication with Allied soldiers, and ran espionage forays on the side. (Derry's false papers, courtesy of Princess Nini and team, declared him an Irish writer employed by the Vatican.)

This network was operating under a regime of martial law, patrolled streets, wiretapped phones, and paid informers. There were betrayals: members were captured and tortured. Most kept their silence, but it was impossible for the rest to know, so each capture necessitated a quiet, desperate flurry of moves to get people to the next haven.

One man in particular honed in on O'Flaherty as a danger to the Reich. Herbert Kappler, chief of the German police and security service in Rome, set the full power of his SS detail on the trail of the elusive monsignor. They set up a comprehensive stalking program to try to catch O'Flaherty on the wrong side of the wide white line painted around the Vatican safety zone, with plans for immediate torture and execution to follow.

That the priest knew he was a target and still calmly took up his scouting post below the basilica in plain view of the SS patrol enraged Kappler. When the flat black hat disappeared, Kappler's men scattered around the perimeter to see where he would surface. But they never seemed to catch on that a coal-man, street sweeper, or – on one or two rumored occasions – a six-foot-two-inch nun might be their person of interest. "He was so charming and for his own safety he couldn't care a damn," recalled Derry.

Kappler's mandate was the obliteration of Roman Jews; he had captured just over two thousand, of whom hardly more than a dozen escaped Auschwitz. So the underground rescue network redoubled its efforts to protect Jews still at liberty. They hid children in religious houses and gave parents false papers.

On at least three documented occasions, Kappler was within snatching distance of his prey; once the man who was supposed to betray O'Flaherty, a former member of his organization, had a last-second change of heart; he looked up into the priest's eyes, and then dodged down a side street. Twice, the monsignor received tip-offs; the last plot included two SS "Mass attendees" who were to follow O'Flaherty out the church door and hustle him across the white line where he could be "shot while attempting escape." John May got wind of that plan, and as the two men stood up after Mass, four Swiss Guards closed in on them. The monsignor continued to hold Mass at the church.

When Allied troops finally marched into Rome on June 4, 1944, the organization had 3,925 escapees in its active care. Postwar research brought the total number aided to approximately 6,500. Meanwhile, O'Flaherty began helping injured Italians and others who had fought for the Axis powers. When called out for "switching sides" he replied, "God has no country."

He didn't care much for the tributes that came his way as his exploits were made known by those who had witnessed them. He never collected his pension awarded by the Italian government. But he did do something else. Every month he stopped by a prison between Naples and Rome where he was the only visitor for one particular inmate: former SS officer Herbert Kappler, convicted of war crimes (most notably the Ardeatine Caves massacre) and sentenced to life in prison. Several years after the war, Kappler requested baptism into the Catholic faith, and O'Flaherty fulfilled his request. ☙

Opposite: A portrait sketch of Monsignor Hugh O'Flaherty believed to have been drawn while he was at the Vatican after his time in Haiti and San Domingo, ca. 1936. Artist unknown.

Photograph courtesy of the Hugh O'Flaherty Memorial Society.